A History of Women
in Medicine

For Grandad

'Woman is the gate of the devil, the path of wickedness, the sting of the serpent, in a word, a perilous object.'

(Saint Jerome, fourth century)

A History of Women in Medicine

Cunning Women, Physicians, Witches

Sinéad Spearing

PEN & SWORD HISTORY

AN IMPRINT OF PEN & SWORD BOOKS LTD
YORKSHIRE - PHILADELPHIA

First published in Great Britain in 2019 by
PEN & SWORD HISTORY
an imprint of
Pen & Sword Books Ltd
Yorkshire – Philadelphia

HB ISBN 978 1 52671 429 9
PB ISBN 978 1 52675 169 0

A CIP catalogue record for this book is available from the British Library

Typeset in Times New Roman 11/13.5 by
Aura Technology and Software Services, India

Printed and bound in the UK by
TJ International, Padstow, Cornwall

Pen & Sword Books Ltd incorporates the imprints of Pen & Sword
Archaeology, Atlas, Aviation, Battleground, Discovery,
Family History, History, Maritime, Military, Naval, Politics, Railways,
Select, Social History, Transport, True Crime, and Claymore Press,
Frontline Books, Leo Cooper, Praetorian Press, Remember When,
Seaforth Publishing and Wharncliffe.

For a complete list of Pen & Sword titles please contact
PEN & SWORD BOOKS LIMITED
47 Church Street, Barnsley, South Yorkshire, S70 2AS, England
E-mail: enquiries@pen-and-sword.co.uk
Website: www.pen-and-sword.co.uk

Or
PEN AND SWORD BOOKS
1950 Lawrence Rd, Havertown, PA 19083, USA
E-mail: Uspen-and-sword@casematepublishers.com
Website: www.penandswordbooks.com

Contents

Special Thanks

A History of Women in Medicine began its life as an idea that refused to live quietly within the structure of my previous book. *Old English Medical Remedies*, published in February of 2018, could not accommodate the lives and practices of the women who used the bizarre array of remedies it contained. So I would like to say thank you to my commissioning editor Jonathan Wright for suggesting a second book might be necessary to do justice to the idea.

When I began my research into the identities of ancient British female physicians, it became clear that the work of archaeologists Helen Meaney and Tania Dickinson was central to my project. To bring these 'cunning-women' alive, not just as an idea but also as living realities within a wider tradition of healing, magic and spiritual practice, was made easier by the tangible evidence discovered by these academics. Thank you, Helen and Tania. Thank you also to the psychologist Jeanne Achterberg for writing *Woman as Healer*, a book that inspired and contributed to the themes within my own. I must also mention Alan Charles Kors and Edward Peters, both of whom inspired me.

This book would never have been published, however, were it not for the wonderful team at Pen and Sword Books. First there is Jonathan Wright who didn't just spot the potential of a burgeoning idea but spotted me also, a year previously, and commissioned my first book. Then there is the wider team including Lauren Burton, Laura Hirst, Jon Wilkinson and others whose names have never reached me but I know are working behind the scenes making an actual book out of my manuscript. A special thanks goes to my editor Carol Trow. Carol has not merely edited my manuscript, turning it from rough to polished but kindly nurtured, advised and picked up my confidence whenever it fell – thank you Carol, you've been amazing.

At home, I have been fortunate to have my feline shadow, Cassie, with me (most) of the time. There are occasions when we battle over who gets to sit in the writer's chair, but she always gives way when treats are offered and then settles down to offer companionship in lonely times. Others close to home are my friend and poet Siân Thomas who read some of my work and gave advice – thank you. I would also like to thank Mark Ripley, of the Robertsbridge Ripleys, who quite literally phoned a friend for the right advice to help me over a bump. Thank you Mark for such a spontaneous act of kindness.

Most of all I want to thank my husband Jeremy Spearing for his invaluable, unwavering support. Also, for acting as first reader and spending many mornings going through page after page of a book about healing, female physicians and witches, when he could have been having a good read of the newspaper. Thank you my love – I'm chuffed to bits you enjoyed it.

Prologue

'Invariably, the deities of the old ways become demons in the new; what was good becomes evil. Woman, as chief representative of the old ways, suffers the consequences as the ancient mother goddess figure is blamed for man's fall from grace. Even the pangs of birth, rather than part of the divine act of producing a miracle, became woman's just deserts.'

Jeanne Achterburg, *Woman as Healer*, 1990

In late May, the small Cotswold village of Bisley stops its daily activities to celebrate an ancient custom. Children dress in old school uniforms from Victorian times and a silver band accompanies their procession through the streets. A celebratory church service then follows, before the crowd of locals carrying flowers and wreaths wends its way through narrow lanes to the ancient village wells.

The locals will readily tell you about this ritual of thanksgiving for the gift of clean water that bubbles up from the earth in seven ancient springs within their village. Thanks are given in the form of flowers, food, colourful banners and other pretty gifts, which are used to decorate the wells. It is a happy day, full of smiles, songs and laughter, with the vicar presiding and offering up prayers.

No one mentions, or perhaps knows, that any prayer offered up 'beside trees or springs … or anywhere except in a church', requires the person to 'do penance for three years on bread and water, since this is a … demonic thing'. At least that was the Church's view in the ninth century according to Halitgar's penitential.

Following the well blessing, life will return to normal in Bisley. No one will fast for penance on bread and water. Demonic collaboration won't be investigated, and women will sleep safe in their beds without fear of the neighbours attacking them with pitchforks, pinning their bodies to the ground and carving crosses into the flesh of their naked chests. A lot has changed since the last such incident in 1945.

Like many customs in the Cotswolds, the tradition of honouring wells and springs goes back to pagan times. Springs did not just give the gift of clean water but were thought by our ancestors to be alive within an animistic cosmology we no longer share. To us it is simply water. To the ancient tribe known as the Hwicce (pronounced 'witchy') who once inhabited the area from Warwickshire to Somerset with the Cotswolds at its heart, springs were living emblems of divine presence within the material world.

The springs of Bisley were sacred places for communion with a living, imminent deity. As spaces within the landscape they were liminal, enchanted places where the natural and supernatural worlds interacted in dialogue and relationship. Magical energies were tangible here and could be used to bring supernatural healing to those sick and suffering.

When Reverend Kemble re-introduced Bisley's well-dressing ceremony in the nineteenth century, few would have believed that Christianity was its source. Yet by this time it was relatively safe to bring back celebrations and rituals that had nurtured the local communities for centuries, although now under the guidance and authority of the Church of course. That the rituals were still well remembered, however, gives insight into the covert continuation of pagan beliefs and practices in the area.

There are countless ancient wells and springs in Hwicce country and all across the United Kingdom that have associations with healing and magic. In the late sixteenth century, a healer named Jonet Boyman used Elrich's Well near Edinburgh as a place to receive guidance for the remedies and prescriptions needed to heal her patients. By calling on 'Blist Benedicte In the name of ye fader and the holye gost', she would see materialised a fairy from the supernatural otherworld who, according to her witch trial testimony, gave her vital information regarding her patient Allan Anderson. She described the fairy as 'wele anewch cled . . . wele faceit wt ane baird'. Despite being a Christian and so praying for advice at the well in the form of the Benedictus, Our Father and Holy Ghost, Jonet, whose only actions had been to relieve the suffering of the sick and help people in times of need, was tortured, tried and burnt as a witch in 1597.

Travelling north from the idyllic Cotswold village of Chipping Campden, there is an old Roman road named Buckle Street. Joining it from the B4632, it runs straight into Bidford-on-Avon. The road was first mentioned in a Saxon charter of 709, where it was called Bugghilde Streete, and again in 967 as Bucgan Streete. Entering Bidford-on-Avon by this road, you cross the river Avon and continue until you see a car park on the right called Saxon Fields.

PROLOGUE

Today, you will find about 45 tarmacked carpark spaces sitting on top of a sixth century Anglo-Saxon graveyard. It was here in 1921, when the road from the bridge was being laid, that around two hundred bodies were found including that of a woman interred at its far edge with items so unusual that archaeologist Tania Dickinson states that this is 'the grave of someone with special powers'. This is quite a statement from an academic researcher, hinting at the very unusual nature of the discovery.

The body is that of a woman who died in Bidford-on-Avon in the early sixth century. Unlike the other bodies that show a degree of poverty, this lady had been buried wearing a long robe with both pagan and Christian brooches and rings. She was further adorned with an elaborate necklace of 39 beads, but what truly sets her apart are the remains of a large bag that hung from her waist containing an unusually long handled knife and antler cone along with organic matter. A leather bib was also evident, upon which was sewn a large number of amuletic pendants. In comparison to her earthy companions, her grave goods suggest she had status within her community.

This large bag, termed a 'doctor's bag' by contemporary researchers, has become an identifying motif of cunning-women (*cunning* meaning 'knowledgeable' in Old English) burials with archeologists Helen Meaney and Tania Dickinson seeing them as evidence of these women's specialisation in medicine, ritual and prophesy.

A particularly fine example of one such bag was discovered in nearby Wheatley, Oxfordshire. From over 70 burials, grave 27 contained many objects; a bag placed beneath the woman's left arm contained a number of glass and amber beads, wolf teeth, a boar's tusk, Roman coins, jewellery and scraps of iron and linen. Between her feet were iron rings, bronze plates and fragments of glass along with a bronze disk, wrist clasp and a peculiar iron rod with a copper wire through one end.

In Winnall, another grave contained the characteristic knife, linen and amulets while at Lechlade, a woman was found buried beneath stones and placed at the far north of the cemetery as if shunned and feared. In Westbury-by-Shenley, a similar bag with an assortment of items including an iron knife, and even a pair of shears accompanied one body and a grave in Abington contained yet another while similar women are being identified from all over Britain and as far away as Germany and Scandinavia. No men are found with objects such as these.

Archaeologists may be providing evidence for what anthropologists have until now only theorised – that women were the physicians in ancient times. This proposal, put forward by Meaney and Dickinson, challenges the widely accepted historic account of medical history, which places medical practice and development firmly in the hands and minds of men. Great names such as Hippocrates and Galen come instantly to mind when pondering medical history. Yet from the earth of ancient Britain, grave goods are painting a very different picture.

Cunning-women healed the sick, prophesied the future and communicated with spiritual beings. They also used what we might call spells and charms to locate lost property and protect people, homes and livestock from harm. Such activities may seem preposterous to us today but in a world where natural occurrences were experienced within a supernatural cosmology, magic was considered a logical tool of agency. Using herbs and metaphysical abilities to heal the sick was the healthcare of the day and from surviving documents it is clear that some of these women were highly skilled physicians and surgeons. From ninth century Old English herbals such as *Bald's Leechbook III* and the *Lacnunga* manuscript we can see their healing work preserved in hundreds of ancient remedies collected in Hwicce territory during the Dark Ages.

Yet a question arises – if these women were respected and knowledgeable physicians, then why do we not know of them? Also, why were they buried at the edges of graveyards and often secured there with piles of stones? The answers are complex, although certain features and signs are beginning to emerge.

Curator Sue Banning from the British Museum for example, sees their demise as a consequence of their special and powerful nature, she says, 'these women were very well respected, but they were quite feared as well. They may have been on the margins of society.' The positioning of their graves supports this theory of an enigmatic yet frightening persona, as archaeologists do indeed find them buried at the edges of cemeteries, often covered with stones or pinned to the ground with iron stakes in a mode of burial usually reserved for murderers.

This book explores these complexities from a unique point of view by asking a further question – why did the name of the Hwicce, the tribe from which so many of these women came, evolve into our Middle English word *'wych'*, and finally resolve into the modern 'witch', and what can this linguistic, symbolic evolution reveal? Also, were these women peculiar to Britain alone or can we trace a wider tradition and belief system into which they belonged? The mythologist Joseph Campbell has, for example, contended that an ancient cult of goddess worship once formed the basis of spiritual practice throughout the ancient world. If he is correct, then perhaps the cunning-women of Britain are a lingering memory of this lost religion with its rituals, hierarchies and celebrations.

Today, the term cunning-woman has been lost from regular parlance and is confused with the loaded term 'witch', mingling herbal healing with notions of evil. It is not easy to speak of these matters at all today without the spectre of witchcraft and witches overshadowing them. The researcher must tread carefully through centuries of controversy, misinformation and deep-rooted prejudices to reveal anything of the real cunning-women beneath the Church's witchcraft propaganda. Yet it is possible to find them. For example, we will see their careers preserved in Old English herbals and their rituals mentioned in old Nordic Sagas. Further evidence from Roman documents even suggests they may have been more than simply healers – Tacitus mentions that the Germanic tribes revered divinely authorised female leaders who were respected politicians, priests and physicians. Are these the same women lying in the ground of ancient Britain?

By teasing out the true identity, persona and lives of cunning-women from the historic record, a very different understanding of witchcraft is consequently revealed from before the word 'witch' conjured images of green skin, hooked noses and unholy unions with the devil. From centuries of attempts to eradicate these so called witches, such as the Augustinian reworking of woman's role in sin, the misogynistic writing of Bishop Prüm, the assimilation of paganism by Pope Gregory and the infamous *Malleus Maleficarum* (and all this before the advent of the witch trials), it becomes clear that condemning them, changing their tribal name to witch, torturing them, burning them and casting their spiritual beliefs as evil has only served to confuse, confound and portray women as lesser creatures than men – a view which persists today.

Feminist writers such as Mary Daly put the subordination of women in today's society firmly at Saint Augustine's door, whereas others argue his view of women was more nuanced. Either way, it can be seen that Augustine was the first to put in place the theory and dogma necessary to battle the veracity of British paganism and the cunning-women who served at the heart of it. His theorising regarding the nature of women enabled the judicial foundation upon which others would build and ultimately deliver the witch trials.

Whether Augustine purposively set out to demonise women is arguable. It seems more likely that his authentic desire to understand the problem of evil produced, as an emergent property, an unfortunate consequence for women – especially those demonstrating any sort of ability towards medicine and spiritual mediation such as the Hwicce physicians of ancient Britain.

Yet the consequences of his work, which puts evil under the auspices of women, led later theologians to develop deeply unsavoury preoccupations with female sexuality. For example, by the twelfth century the Dominican friar Vincent de Beauvais was explaining the nature of women with reference to their anatomy alone – he thought that women were predisposed to carnality and sin because their wombs were unnaturally cold and so they ravenously desired the warmth of a man's semen.

A century later Thomas Aquinas stated in his *Summa Theologica* regarding women that they are 'defective and misbegotten, for the active force in the male seed tends to the production of a perfect likeness in the masculine sex; while the production of woman comes from a defect in the active force or from some material indisposition.'

The *Summa Theologica* was not published until 1485, just two years before Kramer and Sprenger's *Malleus Maleficarum*. The *Malleus* marks in the minds of the most, the beginning of the witch craze. What Kramer achieved with his document was a systemised version of heretical witchcraft that could be justly and rightly brought before the judiciary. His motives, which will be examined later, were far from ethical and his personal penchant for sexual torture equally so.

This book does not document the barbarism. The witch trials are used here to support the focus and themes within the work only. Also, so much has already been written about the trials themselves and at such depth, that there is no need to revisit that well-watered trough here. Suffice it to say, that if any one of us has an ancestor who fell victim to the atrocities of the witch trials, we can be quite sure that they lived and died in unimaginable pain and terror, often with the knowledge they were leaving their loved ones to a similar fate.

A History of Women in Medicine breathes new life into the forgotten world of the Old English female physicians and thereby lifts the cunning-woman of Bidford-on-Avon from her tarmacked grave. Her tribe, her beliefs and her career will be discerned by pulling together a wealth of previously forgotten sources that when combined, present a vivid picture of a class of women that has been denied a voice in the modern world, hidden beneath a contrived fabrication that we know today as the witch. The book follows three general sections: initially the focus is upon the women themselves as archaeological artefacts within a wider social and pagan belief system. Next comes the Church's attitude towards that belief system and the women at its heart before finally, the worlds collide, a battle is waged and the cunning-women are heard from no more – until, a curious nineteenth century clergyman named Oswald Cockayne actually discovered within the Old English herbals *Lacnunga* and *Bald's Leechbook III,* the remedies they had once used.

Cockayne had no idea what he was truly looking at. To him, and all those who have followed, the remedies appeared as little more than barbarian mumbo-jumbo. Lost were voices of the female physicians, the ancient cunning-women, and the subtleties of holistic methods and ancient psychology represented by their herbs and rituals. Cockayne viewed the remedies much as we would today and here is an example of one he read – it is a cure for worms presented here in its original Old English followed by a Modern English translation:

'Ðis ylce galdor mæg mon singan wið smeogan wyrme, sing gelome on ða dolh, ond mid ðinan spatle smyre, ond grene curmeallan, cnuca, lege on þæt dohl, ond beðe mid hattre cumicgan.'

'This same charm may be sung against a burrowing worm, sing often over the sore and smear it with spittle, and take green centaury, pound it, lay it on the sore and bathe it with warm cow's urine.'

The pharmaceutical ingredient used here is the herb centaury, and as the seventeenth century herbalist Nicholas Culpepper explains, 'it kills worms … as is found by experience.' It is a strong bitter and as is true of most bitters, it acts as a vermifuge and so does indeed expel worms. A poultice containing centaury would therefore have had a useful medicinal effect. Less obvious is the use of cow's urine. Yet the medicinal use of cow's urine has been known and used in Ayurvedic medicine for millennia and is used today in Asian medicine and cosmetics, with its benefit supported by specialist research.

The pharmaceutical efficacy of some Old English remedies has been confirmed by students at Nottingham University who, by chance, discovered that a remedy for a *wen* (cyst), cured the super bug MRSA. A whole new area of research has now been born called Ancientbiotics to enable medical researchers to investigate more Old English remedies.

Further to the pharmaceutical herbal ingredients, however, are strange, less familiar directives. In the remedy for worms for example, the physician sings over the wound. Singing and ritual feature often in Old English Hwicce remedies just as they do within the healing practices of surviving shamanic cultures. Song was power, and ritual provided a supernatural landscape where nature's herbs could align with potent spiritual and divine energies to affect healing.

These ritualistic and magical aspects of Old English remedies that have caused clergy, and until recently the medical profession, to dismiss them as nonsensical spells and charms, may however, provide the foundational element for what we today call the placebo effect. The placebo effect is generally understood to be a process of non-medical healing induced by belief alone. Yet, recent research conducted by Harvard University's Dr Cosima Locher, has found that belief may be just one aspect of the mysterious efficacy of the placebo. Dr Locher's study had its participants put their arm onto a hot plate until the pain became too much to bear. The first group received the painkiller lidocaine, the second were told they were receiving a placebo painkiller, and the third group was told they too were receiving a placebo, but this group was also treated to a fifteen-minute personal explanation of the procedure.

The first and third group experienced the same degree of diminished pain leading Dr Locher to conclude that, 'The previous assumption that placebos only work when they are administered by deception needs to be reconsidered.' Also, as the placebo-only group experienced higher pain, the study also found that the doctor/patient relationship, as formulated by the fifteen-minute talk, is of equal importance.

Belief, and the doctor/patient relationship are also central to the remedies in the cunning-women's herbals. Many cures are lengthy and would have required an intimate, relational interaction between physician and patient, sometimes lasting for days at a time. The beliefs of the era such as the power of elves to cause disease and the authority of the divine to thwart them are also evident from the remedies. With this rich tapestry of belief and relationship established, we then find the cunning-woman herself; known for her herbal wisdom and her capacity to mediate with the metaphysical world.

So here is the 'witch's' brew: herbs; knowledge; compassion; supernatural abilities; ritual; and divine mediation. By using these talents and the expectancy her authority in these matters would conjure in the patient's mind, the Bidford-on-Avon cunning-woman was capable of producing a sophisticated form of healthcare that contemporary physicians are only now starting to explore. Healthcare, however, that the Church calls witchcraft.

Chapter 1

From the dust of the ground

Funerary customs and the rites surrounding death and burial offer great insight into the beliefs and lives of ancient cultures. Inhumation is rarely an isolated affair and requires more than just the presence of a corpse. Hidden within the grave goods and the positioning of bodies is an unscripted narrative of meaningful incidents that expose the identities of those involved: there is the family of the deceased with its tribal adherences and regional idiosyncrasies. Also, there are those responsible for deciding the place and mode of burial and others who help to organise and prepare. Finally, there will be those who conduct the ceremony itself while ensuring the whole process aligns with expected and accepted religious traditions. All these factors contribute information that reaches through the centuries to the present day.

Analysing Anglo-Saxon burials and learning the range of customs common to them has allowed archaeologists Audrey Meaney and Tania Dickinson to discern some uncommon phenomena. Particularly, they have found a number of female burials that are different, unique even, and seem to indicate a class of women never before known beyond the world of myth and folklore. Meaney and Dickinson believe they have found the ancient physicians of the day, and these physicians were exclusively women.

In order to appreciate the unusual evidence presented by these archeologists, it is useful to compare it to what has been considered 'normal' in Anglo-Saxon death rites. After all, the people of Anglo-Saxon England had the diverse origins of recent Germanic immigrants and indigenous Britons. It was also the period in British history when Christianity re-established itself, although this was not wholly successful until the seventh century and arguably, much later. As the historian Charles Thomas describes, as late as the seventeenth century, people 'knew more about Robin Hood than they did about the stories in the Bible'. One could be forgiven for wondering therefore, if funerary adherences would not consequently be haphazard or random.

1

Researcher Samantha Lucy has said that there was indeed a 'rich variation' in Anglo-Saxon burials, but she concludes that far from demonstrating a disorganised approach to funerary rites, this demonstrates that the Anglo-Saxons took their death rites seriously and experienced them as meaningful. Variety does not necessarily indicate randomness but rather, it reveals that funerary motifs surrounding the objects and circumstances of burial reflected the gender, wealth and status of the individual within their wider cultural context.

Anglo-Saxon burials are distinct from earlier Roman and Iron Age ones. The invaders brought their culture and religion with them and although their early burials show some Romano-British features due to a lingering Celtic heritage, most are specifically identifiable as Anglo-Saxon, albeit with regional differences according to tribal and continental influences. Yet one thing is true of the Anglo-Saxons' relationship to their dead – within their poetry and funerary rites we find a deep reverence for those who have died, as Sonia Chadwick Hawkes describes when speaking of the Finglesham cemetery in Kent:

> 'Abandoned homes rarely yield more than building foundations and the kinds of objects people threw away. Their cemeteries on the other hand, contain the things treasured by the Anglo-Saxons, their mortal remains and the precious possessions which they sought to take with them after death.'

Death and burial were important processes and during this time, we find both burial and cremation being used, although as Christianity took hold the cremations recede. Village graveyards of poor Anglo-Saxon communities have been overshadowed in the popular arena by the extravagantly impressive treasure hoards unearthed at sites such as Sutton Hoo. More recently, a huge array of treasure was discovered in a potato field in Lincolnshire. Here, a particularly fine example of an amuletic pendant was found, made of gold and highly polished deep red garnet. Before silvered glass mirrors, these darkly polished pendants created a black mirror and were used to deflect the evil eye and protect the wearer from harm.

The Finglesham site is a good example of a standard Anglo-Saxon cemetery. It is in an elevated position surrounded by ancient springs and separated from the earlier Roman graveyard in the area. There are a number of small mound burials denoting people of status and many more common graves. Women were generally buried with combs, jewellery, tweezers and keys. Men never have keys, as women were the head of the household and the keys were symbolic of their role. Men were commonly buried with weapons; knives for poorer folk through to swords, spears and shields for the more well off, who also had coffins of wood. For the very wealthy, the casket could be lead lined.

There are therefore a number of expected elements within Anglo-Saxon burials, despite regional differences. Yet curiosities begin to emerge when we look at the positioning of certain corpses. Bodies are normally found lying on their backs (supine) or sides with their grave goods around them. According to anthropologist Nick Stoodley, however, about one per cent of bodies are found in rather different circumstances that have led researchers to term them 'deviant'. Andrew Reynolds uses the terms 'prone' (face down) to identify many of these burials. Commonly believed to be the graves of those outcast from society, the term deviant is both illuminating and descriptive, referring to those considered different in some way. It could be someone who departed from the accepted standards or expectations of society or those who engaged in unlawful behaviours. Reynolds explains:

'In the pre-Christian centuries Early Anglo-Saxon communities arguably marked the burials of people considered somehow different, and perhaps dangerous to the living, in distinctive ways, and certain of these locally determined but widely understood modes of treating social 'others' can be observed to continue until the nineteenth century in England.'

This way of treating social 'others' can also be seen in burial customs pre-dating the Anglo-Saxons. Roman, Iron Age, as well as funerary examples from other parts of the world, mark the passing of so called deviants with distinctive methods of burial or cremation. Yet Reynolds also uses the word 'dangerous' in his comment. One would have thought, however, that any danger posed in life from the individual would cease to cause concern upon their death. But due to superstitions and beliefs of the time, this was not the case.

The dead held great power for our ancestors as is evidenced by a lineage of ancestor worship, where loved ones were viewed as still existent and capable of intervening, to a degree, within the lives of the living. It is therefore reasonable to assume that people who were not loved ones, or worse, were deviant or dangerous during their earthly lives, might be similarly viewed as capable of continuing to inflict their aberrant behaviour upon those left behind. Archaeological findings from these strange inhumations would certainly suggest so. Stakes through the heart, post-mortem decapitations, hobbling and corpses weighed down in the earth by stones are just some of the methods our ancestors used to ensure that the corpse could not rise to cause harm upon the living.

Near the village of Chadlington in Oxfordshire, there is an Anglo-Saxon graveyard of around 50-60 burials. The grave goods are sparse, indicating that this was a poor community and as far as graveyards go, there is little to report. Yet two men, in graves numbered 9 and 10 were found decapitated, with their heads placed between their knees. Reynolds has noted that Oxfordshire along with neighbouring Gloucestershire and also Worcestershire and Somerset (all fall within ancient Hwicce territory) contain particularly significant clusters of these types of inhumation.

Nottinghamshire also has a few striking deviant burials, one of which came to the popular media's attention in 2012 when researchers discovered that a sixth century skeleton from Southwell had been interred with metal stakes thrust through each shoulder blade, each ankle and finally, through the heart. This ancient man has become known affectionately in the locale as the Medieval Vampire, although his mode of burial would suggest less affection was held for him whilst alive.

Archaeology is not the only evidence for these burials and beliefs. In Heinrich Kramer's *Malleus Maleficarum* of 1487, he uses the story of an old woman accused of witchcraft to make clear to his audience the real and present danger posed to the living by suspected witches who had died.

Kramer describes a case where a small German town was being abandoned due to the population dying. An alleged witch was thought to be the cause as she had been buried with no protective devices to prevent her from causing harm to the living. A rumour was circulating that the old woman was somehow still alive within the grave, eating her own burial cloth, and all the while she did so, people would die. Panic was rising, people were either dying or starting to leave and no one, so it seems, gave any thought to a cause other than necromantic witchcraft. In desperation, the town officials decided to dig the old woman up, and when they did so they discovered, so it stated, that about half the linen cloth was indeed eaten and visible within the rotting gullet of the old spinster. They cut off the corpse's head with a sword and, so the tale goes, according to Kramer, the deathly plague immediately ceased.

Archaeologists Meaney and Hawkes have found 'stoning' to be an enduring tradition in relation to deviant burials. Stoning refers to a process where the corpse is literally weighted down by a mass of stones and boulders. They state in their 1970 work *Two Anglo-Saxon Cemeteries at Winnall,* that similarities in this type of burial occur in Scandinavia where folklore not only retains the knowledge that inhumations performed in this way were to 'lay the ghosts of criminals, but also against any other person who, it was feared, might have a grievance against the living.'

The term 'deviant' may, however, be misleading. Although Reynolds is correct and most of these burials seem to indicate criminals and those outcast from society, the work of Meaney and Dickinson is demonstrating a sub category within this type of inhumation that does not relate to criminal or aberrant behaviours. Instead, some graves currently marked out as deviant might fulfil a rather different category of inhumation with specific magical, healing motifs that indicate the deceased to be something other than the scorned, reviled corpses contained within deviant graves.

Meaney and Dickinson's theory regarding a new category of deviant burial centres on the grave goods accompanying certain women. Unlike the criminal burials, these women often have objects denoting status, wealth and respect, leading Meaney to suggest that these graves evidence a unique class of women. Within their graves we discover in addition to the expected items of jewellery, combs and needles the unexpected inclusion of bags and pouches containing organic materials, spices, linen bandages and peculiar objects of magical significance alone.

Helen Geake has argued that 'almost every type of Anglo-Saxon female grave-good has, at one time or another, been identified as possessing amuletic or magical significance', however, Meaney noticed that within these female burials there were nonetheless too many items of a non-utilitarian nature suggestive of healing and magic. She decided to call this new category of Anglo-Saxon female burials 'cunning-women' to denote their position as healers, from the Old English *cunnende* meaning 'to know'. Yet this is not a new designation, as we see the term cunning-woman used in the Middle Ages to describe folk-healers. Today, we prefer the word wise-woman, as 'cunning' has evolved to mean sly and surreptitious behaviour.

Archaeology has therefore identified that a number of women with deviant burials do indeed have a class of grave goods distinct from other inhumations. But how can we truly know these objects are those of a cunning-woman or Old English healer as Meaney and Dickinson contend? Could they not indicate another role for these women that we as yet do not understand? Without more evidence, the theory of female physicians or cunning-women remains speculative. The grave goods such as antler cones, tiny tubes, shears, linens, amulets, iron rods and scalpel knives which point to non-utilitarian use have not yet been verified as medico-magical tools or contextualised within a working understanding of ancient healing - until now.

Chapter 2

Flesh on the Bones

The cunning-woman of Bidford-on-Avon exists today as little more than bones. Even her grave goods can only tell a partial story of who she might have been. Her medicine bag and further unusual items are intriguing, yet with nothing more to add to the picture, an element of speculation remains.

Sixth century Bidford-on-Avon was home to an Anglo-Saxon community of farmers. Animal enclosures and postholes from dwellings reveal a poor community leading modest lives. The men reared livestock and women wove and ground corn – loom weights have been found in the earth along with quern stones. This was a hand-to-mouth existence constantly overshadowed by the threat of disease and hunger. Only the cunning-woman stands out as different, out of place, in this otherwise domestic rural scene.

Burial number HB2 is the only identification of this otherwise unknown woman. Yet for the first time it is now possible to speak with some certainty regarding her life, beliefs and activities although to do so with some meaning and respect requires a more personal designation than HB2. So, for ease of discussion the name Mildþryþ (pronounced similarly to the modern Mildred) is given to her here. Mildþryþ is an Anglo-Saxon female name meaning kingly and wise.

Archaeology alone cannot resurrect Mildþryþ from her tarmacked grave. Her clothes, such as the lavish robe and ornate jewellery, do create some clarity, and add to this her height of 5 feet 4 inches and her age of between 18 to 24 years and the door opens a little wider. Religion is often a useful marker within identity and as the cemetery where she was discovered was pagan Saxon, we can also discern something of her beliefs. Now, include detailed documentation regarding the day-to-day activities and methods of her career, and the door stands wide.

Contemporary psychologists such as Vladimir Skorikov have described how personal identity and a sense of self are developed and exposed most powerfully in relation to the activities we engage with in our careers and vocations. Although we should be cautious in layering modern psychological theory onto the pre-medieval mind, we may at least interpret that mind into a semblance of personhood useful for us today. We can, to a degree, bring Mildþryþ back to life.

Mildþryþ and her grave goods continue to puzzle archeologists today, indeed the 'Windows on Warwickshire' website, which presents her grave goods and speculates that Mildþryþ may be a wise-woman, seeks help in solving the mystery. They ask for example – 'What use would the antler cone have?' Their team of researchers then put forward potential answers such as a drinking vessel, amulet or pendant. These ideas are logical, as the Anglo-Saxons held horn in high esteem, believing it to be imbued with the health and vitality of the beast from which it came and so horns were often used to make drinking vessels.

The true answer emerges, however, from studying and deciphering a ninth century monastic manuscript written in Hwicce territory and based in part on an earlier work from the sixth century. The text is known as *Bald's Leechbook III* (healing book III), and along with its slightly later companion piece *Lacnunga* (Remedies) contains medicinal remedies identified in *Old English Medical Remedies* (2018) as being of uniquely British origin.

Bald's Leechbook III was commissioned by *Ælfheah the Bald*, Bishop of Winchester, for reasons that ultimately remain mysterious. Perhaps he decided to collect together the indigenous remedies from local cunning-women such as *Mildþryþ* as a competitive strategy to take clients away from local healers to enrich the ever-growing monastic coffers – or perhaps he had been inspired by King Alfred's (Alfred means 'Wise Elf' in Old English) plan to form a united England and added to the process a medical handbook of indigenous British remedies – the flora and fauna of local plants would certainly serve the population better than those of the Mediterranean herbals commonly used by the clergy. Whatever the cause of the Bishop's decision, his collection of remedies in *Bald's Leechbook III* stands as testament to the work of cunning-women and resurrects Mildþryþ's career, bringing forth her voice. *Bald's Leechbook III* and *Lacnunga,* for ease of narrative, will be referred to as Mildþryþ's books and remedies in the current work.

From the many documented remedies in Mildþryþ's books, there are a number that include the type of antler horn found buried with her. Although the cures are written in Old English and require careful research to clarify scribal errors, and mistakes made in previous translations, when the work is done the mystery of Mildþryþ's grave goods are resolved and her identity as a physician confirmed. As an example of this process of deciphering, take the following remedy for an eye cream:

'Eahsealf, win ond piper, do in horn ond in þa eagan þonne þu restan wille.'

'Eyesalve, wine and pepper, put in a horn and into the eyes when you wish to rest a while.'

The horn is used in this remedy as an administering device for an eye salve. Mildþryþ's horn had holes in each end – it was also small and stubby and would have served well to drop ointment into specific places like the eyes, nose and ears. Yet when considering the ingredients and intention of the remedy, something seems odd.

Firstly, a salve would not drip through the horn as easily as an ointment. Salves feature often in the Mildþryþ's remedies and are always made with some form of carrier such as fat or butter, yet no such carrier is mentioned here. Also, the active ingredients of pepper and wine are peculiar for an eye remedy – whether a salve or not, putting alcohol and pepper directly into the eye would probably do more harm than good. Both would irritate and burn the delicate membranes. We are left for the moment therefore, with an unsatisfactory cure.

At this point, it was necessary to refer back to the original document held in the British Library to check for errors. It was immediately obvious from the Old English text that the word for 'eye salve' was problematic – the scribe has written *eah,* and *eah* is not a word. It seemed probable that this was a spelling mistake, which the first translator of the document, a priest named Oswald Cockayne guessed at, and all future researchers who reply upon his translation, continue to use. Oswald, it seems, thought the scribe meant *eag*, which is the Old English for 'eye'. Had Oswald analysed the content of the remedy, however, rather than simply translating it, he might have preferred to solve the spelling mistake as *ear*, which also means 'ear' in Old English.

If we re-read the remedy, inserting ear for eye, then things become clear. Dripping a mixture of wine and pepper into the ear through an antler horn is more convincing. Also, alcohol combined with vinegar or pepper is still used today to loosen earwax and relieve aching. It is by this type of detective work that Mildþryþ's grave goods can be proven to be of medicinal purpose.

A second remedy, this time for a cough also uses an antler cone:

'Wiþ hwostan, genim swegles æppel ond swefl ond recels, ealra emfela, meng wiþ weaxe, lege on hatne stan, drine þurh horn þone rec ond ete æfter ealdes spices iii snæda oððe butran ond supe mid fletum.'

'For a cough, take a ball of swail, and sulphur, and incense, equal amounts of each, mix with wax, lay it onto a hot stone, inhale the smoke through a horn, and let him eat three pieces of old bacon or butter afterwards, sip it with curds.'

This cure sets a scene where one might imagine the young Mildþryþ, dressed to impress in her fine robe, jewellery and doctor's bag hanging from her waist. She encounters someone wishing to know about her prescriptions – a monk from Winchester's scriptorium perhaps, or, if this remedy survives from the sixth century then an early researcher, intent on learning her medical skills:

'And what of general complaints?' he might have asked, 'the coughs and colds that plague us all?'

'*Wiþ hwostan?*' (For a cough?) she replies, 'Ah, well let me tell you what I would do. *Genim swegles æppel...* ' (Take a ball of swail...).

A second relationship also emerges from this remedy – a patient is to be visited – someone is suffering with a cough and given that the physician has been called, we might assume it is persistent and troublesome. Upon entering the dwelling of her patient, Mildþryþ would have been greeted with intense smoke from a fire burning in the hearth. After a conversation and some diagnostic investigations, she would then have taken swail, sulphur and further dried herbs from her doctor's bag and kindled them with wax on a heated stone. When the herbs and sulphur were producing smoke, she would take the antler horn from her medicinal tools and help her patient to inhale the vapours. The bacon, butter and curds were probably her postscript:

'Now you make sure you eat three pieces of bacon or butter, and then sip some curds. You'll soon be well.'

Today we might inhale eucalyptus when we have a cough or cold, but here sulphur, swail and incense are prescribed. We don't know what the incense might consist of – perhaps at the time of collecting these remedies the ingredients were simply widely known or alternatively, secret.

Swail (a form of meadow grass) would have acted as a good kindling agent for the mixture. But sulphur is an odd ingredient to find in a remedy for a cough. When researching sulphur inhalation today you will discover that it is poisonous and irritating to the nose and lungs, which seems counter-intuitive within a cure for a cough.

Yet inhaling sulphur has been used as an immune system restorative for thousands of years and can be found in ancient Egyptian remedies. In small quantities, perhaps combined with other soothing vapours from the incense, the sulphur may be used here to mimic the experience of hot sulphurous springs that have long been known for their health benefits, bringing many trace elements and minerals to the body. Hot springs were certainly in existence at the time and place, as the baths of Bath indicate.

Eating three pieces of bacon or butter would give a useful protein boost with the number three symbolic of wholeness and health. The Anglo-Saxons revered a Trinitarian goddess known as the Fates or Norns who watched over the lives of mankind and created destinies by weaving webs of fate. The Trinity, like the later Trinity of Christianity was a powerful symbiotic relationship between three characters of one deity and when invoked, was thought to bring divine assistance to the ritual of healing.

Eating curds might well provide a soothing mucosal element for a sore, irritated throat and combined with the bacon and butter could be similar to the idea of chicken soup today. Often thought to be little more than an old-wives' tale, contemporary research has noted the benefits of chicken soup for the common cold, from its immune support to the improved function of the tiny nasal hairs that prevent infections from spreading further than the nose. From the ingredients prescribed, it could be suggested that this remedy is not just for a cough, but includes elements that also treat the causal immune deficiency of a more generalised cold or bronchial infection.

The Anglo-Saxons had a variety of words to describe the sniffling symptoms of a cold. A particularly satisfying one defined in the Bosworth-Toller Dictionary of Old English as being 'full of snivel, having a cold in the head' is *snoflig.*

Open almost any page within Mildþryþ's books and you will find remedies and potions to cure all manner of mundane ailments such as coughs, headaches, sore eyes, earaches and bronchial congestion. It seems common colds, *snoflig* and the flu were just as debilitating to Mildþryþ's patients as they can be for us and they sought relief from women such as Mildþryþ just as we would from our doctor or pharmacist.

The houses and lives of residents in Bidford-on-Avon from the fifth to ninth centuries changed little. This small farming community touched time infrequently and only the life and death of family members and the passing of the harvest and festivals would have marked it with certainty. Illness, even minor complaints such as coughs, held the hidden fear of sudden complications and another death to add to the journey of time. Mildþryþ's role in the lives of these people cannot be underestimated.

Mildþryþ is unlikely to be the actual person in dialogue with the collectors of these remedies; her presence here is emblematic of the tradition of physicians in the Hwicce tribe who became demonised as witches in later centuries. Given the time, place and mode of healing suggested in the remedies, which researchers such as Debby Banham have identified as uniquely British, it is nonetheless probable that Mildþryþ's voice remains discernible. One of her colleagues or even a student or descendant of Mildþryþ herself could have been the source of *Bald's Lecchbook III:*

> 'Although English vernacular medicine of the late ninth to twelfth centuries draws heavily upon the classical and sub-classical tradition, classical authorities are almost never cited. In fact, citations of any kind are very rare, and the majority of authorities cited in texts compiled before the Norman Conquest are themselves English. Only in the twelfth century are Galen and Hippocrates mentioned for the first time. This suggests a rather self-sufficient medical community in England, with limited historical awareness or contact with wider developments.'
>
> (Debby Banham, *Dun, Oxa and Pliny the Great Physician*, 2011.)

Chapter 3

The 'Doctor's Bag'

'The girl said, "Let me see thy wound, and I will bind it." Thereupon Thormod sat down, cast off his clothes, and the girl saw his wounds, and examined that which was in his side, and felt that a piece of iron was in it, but could not find where the iron had gone in. In a stone pot she had stirred together leeks and other herbs, and boiled them, and gave the wounded man of it to eat, by which she discovered if the wounds had penetrated into the belly; for if the wound had gone so deep, it would smell of leek.'

Heimskringla, Snorri Sturluson, ca. 1230.

The Old English healing books of Mildþryþ detail the remedies used by cunning-women but they are not particularly descriptive. Here, however, in Snorri Sturluson's chronicles of the Norwegian Kings, which is extensively considered an historic source for Saxon and Viking information, a scene is in motion where both the physician and patient are participating in a healing event. The wound to be cured, the diagnostic process and medical relationship create a window into an intimate moment where a poet warrior is seeking help from 'the girl'. This is not just the girl next door – by observing the digestive process and drawing on her olfactory sense, this girl is seeking to ascertain whether the man's gut is perforated. A degree of expertise and knowledge may be inferred here.

After her diagnosis one might then imagine the following type of intervention as we find within Mildþryþ's repertoire of remedies:

'Gif men sie innelfe ute, gecnua galluc, awring þurh cla∂ on cu wearme meolce, wæt þine handa þæron ond gedo þæt innelfe on þone man, geseowe mid seolce, wyl him þonne galluc nygan morgans butan him leng þearf sie, fed hine mid fersce hænneflæsc.'

'If someone's bowels be out, pound comfrey, wring it out into a cloth into warm cow's milk, wet your hands thereon and put the

12

bowel back into the man, sew it together with silk, boil the comfrey
for him for nine mornings unless longer be needful to him, feed
him with hen's flesh.'

One could easily imagine 'the girl' continuing her work by dipping her hands into comfrey-imbued milk and sewing the wound shut with silk. Silk sutures would have dissolved over time and if infection was avoided, then this surgical procedure may have proven successful. Avoidance of infection seems to be paramount in Mildþryþ's mind as she coats her hands with the mixture of comfrey and milk. Today, research has demonstrated the anti-bacterial and anti-viral properties of proteins found in fresh unpasteurised milk. Of comfrey, it was said by the herbalist Culpepper that:

'The root boiled in water or wine and the decoction drank, heals inward hurts, bruises, wounds and ulcers…. A syrup made there of is very effectual in inward hurts, and the distilled water for the same purpose also, and for outward wounds or sores in the fleshy or sinewy parts of the body,'

Culpepper further states that the roots of the plant are more beneficial than the leaves. Unfortunately, we cannot know for sure which part of the herb Mildþryþ used in the remedy, although she does instruct that the tonic should be boiled each morning for a period of nine days, or longer if needed. Mildþryþ would not have simply disappeared from her patient's dwelling. Healing could be a lengthy affair and patient and physician might have become well acquainted.

Tania Dickinson described Mildþryþ's 'doctor's bag' as containing a 'surgical knife', so the type of surgical vignette proposed above may have been part of a cunning-woman's duties. As a physician, Mildþryþ saw patients and diagnosed their illnesses and as a pharmacologist she also made drugs and supervised their applications. There are few instances of surgical procedures in Mildþryþ's books, yet enough evidence survives to show that cunning-women fulfilled this altogether more specialist task.

The knife discovered in Mildþryþ's doctor's bag has a peculiarly long wooden handle with evidence of artistic carving, and a short scalpel-like blade at one end. The blade is indeed tiny and it is difficult to see how it would have served as either a weapon, or as an instrument for slicing herbs. Within the catalogue of Mildþryþ's remedies, however, there is an unpleasant minor surgical procedure that must have required such a tool:

'Gif wyrmas sien on eagum scearpa þa bræwas innan, do on þa scearpan celeþonian seaw, þa wyrmas bioþ deade ond þa eagan hale.'

'If worms be in the eyes, score inside the eyelids, put celandine juice into the cuts, the worms will be dead and the eyes healthy.'

The blade required to score inside the patient's eyelids must have been small and scalpel-like. Mildþryþ then drips celandine juice into the cuts, perhaps using the antler horn. Celandine has been used in eye cures for centuries. It is also used internally today to boost the immune system and calm the nerves. Mentioned by the Greek pharmacologist Dioscorides in the first century, it continued to find favour throughout Anglo-Saxon Britain and was stated in John Gerard's 1597 herbal as being useful as 'it cleanseth and consumeth away slimie things that cleave about the ball of the eye and hinder the sight'. 'Slimie things' that 'cleave' around the eyeball might refer to worms.

Almost all of Mildþryþ's cunning-woman colleagues have been discovered buried with knives, but none so uniquely fine and specialised as Mildþryþ's. It may be that surgery was reserved for the most talented cunning-woman, a consultant of sorts, specialising in this difficult, challenging area of medicine. Of the other knives discovered, most are more utilitarian in nature and may have used for chopping herbs and carving roots as this cure for haemorrhoids shows:

'Wið ðone bledendan fic, nim murran ða wyrt, ond ceorf of nygan penegas ond do on ælcne hunig ond ðige ða on æfen on deft oðre nygann mergen, ond do swa nigon dagas ond nygan niht butan ðe raðorbot cume.'

'Against the bleeding fig, take the herb myrrh and carve off nine pennyweights and put honey on each, and then eat them in the evening and again another nine in the morning, do again for nine days and nine nights unless it is cured sooner.'

The number nine, being three times three, was important for the Anglo-Saxons. It forms the main ritualistic element in this cure and would have invoked within the imagination of the physician and patient alike, the authority and intercedence of the Trinitarian goddess to augment the power of the herbs.

Myrrh is an unusually exotic ingredient for an Old English remedy and although the plant was available in Anglo-Saxon Britain it was used predominantly for coughs and sore throats – it continues to be used as an expectorant today. Also, myrrh has anti-bacterial and anti-inflammatory properties and has been used topically on sores, ulcers and haemorrhoids for centuries.

If the pieces of myrrh covered in honey were applied directly to the haemorrhoid, some benefit might be afforded. Yet Mildþryþ is recommending an internal prescription here. Using myrrh internally was rare, although it is documented in medieval times that tonics to promote digestion and cure parasites contained the resin. In December's issue of the 1989 *New Scientist,* Dr Colin Michie reported that biochemists have recently found that the resins in myrrh are composed of flavonoids that reduce inflammation and enhance immune response so myrrh may 'still find a place in today's therapeutic armoury'. Perhaps Mildþryþ is using the plant internally here for non-protruding piles – those not easily reached by topical applications.

One of the strangest references to knives comes specifically from *Bald's Leechbook III* and concerns a remedy to thwart elf-sickness. The inclusion of creatures such as elves, devils and nightwalkers often point to what we today understand to be psychological or neurological issues such as schizophrenia or epilepsy.

Our ancestors saw the more psychological and neurological aspects of illness as the work of outside agents such as elves. This was because to them, the causality of such complaints could not be deduced and this lack of understanding led to feelings of hopelessness. We can only imagine for example, how disarming and terrifying it must have been in the sixth to ninth centuries to witness or experience an epileptic seizure. For a seemingly healthy person to suddenly fall to the ground in the grip of a seizure must have seemed like a strike from the gods, or in this case, elves:

'Wiþ ælfadle, gang on æfen þonne sunne on setle sie þær þu wite elenan standan, sing þonne benedicte.... ond stibg þin seax on þa wyrte, læt stician þæron, gang þe aweg, gang eft to þonne dæg ond niht furþum scade, on þa ilcan, uhte gang ærest to ond þe gesena ond gode þe bebeod, gang þonne swigende ond þeah þe hwæthwega egeslices ongean cume, oððe man, ne cweþ þu him æny word to ær þu cume to þære wyrte þe þu on æfen ær gemearcodest... adelf þa wyrt, læt stician þæt seax þæron, gang eft swa þu raþost mæge to ciricean ond lege under weofod mid þam seaxe, læt licgean oþ þæt

sunne uppe sie, awæsc siþþan, do to dreanc ond bisceopwyrt....
awyl þriwa on meolcum,'

*'For elf-sickness, go on Wednesday evening when the sun is setting
where you know dwarf elder to be standing, sing the benedicte ...
stab your knife into the plant, let it stick thereon, then go away,
then go again when day and night divide at dawn, then on the
same day, at twilight go first and sign yourself, and bid good for
yourself, then go in silence, and no matter what frightful thing
or man should come towards you say no word to him before you
come to the plant which you marked on the previous evening ...
dig out the plant, let the knife remain there, let it lie there until the
sun comes up, afterwards wash it and make it into a drink, and
betony ... boil them three times in milk.'*

The Old English word for knife is *seax* which describes any blade from
a small utility knife to a fighting weapon. This is an involved remedy
requiring a number of steps and directives. We can begin to see from this
complexity that for the ancient cunning-women, healing was about more
than just pharmaceutical herbal ingredients. A wider landscape is apparent
here where the days, such as Wednesday (Woden's Day), the time of sunset
and dawn, the role of silence and the ritualistic use of the knife all converge
to create a rich and powerful healing experience.

These more ritualistic elements might lack empirical validity, but the
wealth of such material from Mildþryþ's books indicates that such activities
were believed to be meaningful. Whether such magical notions actually
work or are just a placebo continues to be an area of contemporary debate.
Stewart Williams in his 2004 paper *The Placebo Effect*, defines it as:

'a genuine psychological or physiological effect, in a human or
another animal, which is attributable to receiving a substance or
undergoing a procedure, but is not due to the inherent powers of
that substance or procedure.'

Modern medicine is only just beginning to take this seemingly magical
process seriously. A 2014 BBC *Horizon* documentary described the
placebo as the 'medicine in our minds' and reported new research
demonstrating how patients undergoing faux spinal surgery, where they
believed a procedure had taken place when it hadn't, experienced profound,
quantifiable recovery.

Yet the 'trick' of the placebo, which has been theorised to be a powerful type of belief, may not be the whole story: in a 2010 study conducted by Harvard professor Ted Kaptchuk, it was found that IBS sufferers who were clearly told that their tablets were fake, even to the degree that the word 'placebo' was written on the bottle, experienced a statistically significant improvement in their symptoms. Deception was not necessary for the placebo effect to work, therefore belief is only one aspect of the phenomenon. Kaptchuk concluded that 'these findings suggest that rather than mere positive thinking, there may be significant benefit to the very performance of medical ritual.'

Physician Max Clyne further describes how the relationship between the doctor and patient is the most important aspect of the 'medical ritual'. Clyne even puts forward a theory of 'doctor as placebo', to clarify the significance of this ritualised relational encounter in the process of healing. Building upon this idea, neuroscientist Fanbrizio Benedetti has also discovered how the relationship between physician and patient triggers 'intricate psychological factors' that collapse the dualism between biology and psychology providing a ripe framework for mind-body healthcare.

A further item from Mildþryþ's doctor's bag that has until now defied explanation is the array of tiny metal cylindrical tubes. It has been suggested by the 'Windows on Warwickshire' historical team that these might have been used for the ends of her leather thong fastenings, rather like the plastic tubes we find on laces today. This is a possibility, yet if true then we might expect to find many more such tubes in a variety of graves, and we simply do not.

Yet within Mildþryþ's remedies we find a reference to tubes like these, in this case cylindrical reeds, being used for healing a burrowing worm:

> 'Wið smeawyrme smiring, nim swines geallan ond fisces geallan ond hrefnes geallan ond haran geallan, meng to somne, smire þa dolh mid, blaw mid hreoden þæt seaw on þæt dolh, cnua þonne heorot brembel leaf, lege on þa dolh.'

> *'Against a burrowing worm, an ointment, take pig's gall and fish's gall and raven's gall and hare's gall, mix them together, smear the wound with it, blow the juice onto the wound through a reed, then pound hart bramble's leaf, lay it on the wound.'*

Reeds offer an immediate tube-like tool and if these were commonly part of a healer's kit, then they would not have survived in the ground to inform us today. It is possible, however, that a healer of some renown and wealth, such as Mildþryþ, might well have enjoyed rather more superior medical implements than most. Using the humble reed might have been beneath her status. Carefully made tubes of metal or bone could have made more worthy additions to her specialist's bag.

An overlooked item of Mildþryþ's grave goods are the assortment of iron pieces or 'scraps'. No one knows what these were used for and speculation has thought them potentially talismanic. Yet in the next remedy for skin eruptions and boils, we see such instruments being used to heat water, 'gehæt ceald wæter mid isenen, ond beþe mid gelome.' *(heat cold water with iron and bathe it often)*.

The above is one small directive in a long list of advice from Mildþryþ's books for dealing with erupting boils. Applying warm water to boils and abscesses has long been known to help draw infected material to the surface of the skin. In the manuscript, the preceding prescription recommends burning a swallow's nest together with dung and smearing the boil with it. The heat from the poultice of dung and fibres probably served a similar purpose to the water above.

Scraps of iron, heated in the fire and put into a container of cold water may well have sufficed for this particular prescription. If one were to imagine a specifically formulated tool for the job, however, an iron rod such as that found with another Hwicce cunning-woman from Wheatley, Oxfordshire might be perfectly designed. She was interred with an iron rod that has a copper wire threaded through its top like a hoop. It is just the right length for placing in a pot of water and the copper hoop would make it easier to lift it in and out of the hot coals and manoeuvre it into the water, submerging and removing it as required. The discarded iron scraps may thus have had a use for heating water.

Textiles are by far the most frequently mentioned medicinal tools in the Old English texts. Similarly, fabric is the most prevalent item discovered in the graves of cunning-women. For years the humble fragments of linen were simply thought to be remnants of a woman's traditional work of sewing and weaving.

The emerging field of cognitive archaeology contends, however, that items within burials, touched and created by human hands, often have greater significance than the utility we might ascribe to them today. Daily tools are particularly emblematic when they become ritual objects, placed carefully within the landscape of mortality, accompanying an individual to the grave. They exist as both material and spiritual markers from the person's life.

So, according to theorists such as Dupont, the large amounts of thread and textiles discovered with Mildþryþ and other cunning-women cannot be random. Linen must have formed part of Mildþryþ's daily ritual within her life and career, and as Christina Lee explains:

> 'In the case of the woman from Bidford-on-Avon, she had a bag... filled with textile fragments... Bags, satchels, and other containers are not unusual in burial, but in the case of the cunning-women, such bags may be assumed to be the equivalent of modern "doctor's bags". These burials also show that textiles were used in spiritual and physical healing processes, and that there may have been a special person with medical and pharmacological knowledge.'

(Christina Lee, Threads and Needles: The Use of Textiles for Medical Purposes, 2016.)

From Mildþryþ's work we find this assortment of textiles reflected in her remedy descriptions as she deals with all manner of healthcare interventions and pharmacological processes with a humble piece of linen cloth:

> 'Wyrc gode dolhsealfe, nim gearwan ond wudurofan nioþowearde, feldmoran ond nioþweardne sigelhweorfan, wyl on godre buteran, awring þurh clað ond læt gestanden, wel ælc dolh þu meaht lacnian mid.'

> *'Make a good wound salve, take yarrow and the lower part of dog rose, parsnip and the lower part of sun-turner, boil in good butter, wring out through a cloth and let it stand. You can heal every wound well with it.'*

This remedy is for a salve to cure a wound and there are many similar to this in the manuscripts. Here the ingredients, yarrow, dog rose, parsnip and sun-turner (sunflower), are being boiled in butter and wrung through the cloth to produce a salve. We are told it will heal all wounds well and so it is likely this was a general 'go to' remedy for skin trauma. Sunflower has a long tradition of being used to treat haemorrhoids and yarrow has been used for calming the skin. Parsnip is good for sores and dog rose is an anti-inflammatory. All these ingredients would have offered some calming relief for a wound although without any discernable antiseptic qualities.

We may assume that a wound like this would also have required binding, with linen acting as a bandage and although this is not mentioned in the above remedy, we find it in a cure from the *Lacnunga* text for a wound that will not stop bleeding:

'Gif þu ne mæge bloddolh forwriþan nim niwe horses tord, adrig on sunnan, gegnid to duste swiþe wel, lege þæt dust swiþe þicce on linenne claþ, wriþ mid þy þæt dolh.'

If you be unable to staunch a bleeding wound, take fresh horse droppings, dry them out in the sun, crush very thoroughly to dust, lay the dust on a linen cloth very thickly, bind the wound with it.

Some of the items in this remedy hardly require the translation. Horse droppings (*horses tord*), dust (*duste*) and linen cloth (*linenne claþ)* are pleasantly similar to our modern words. The linen is employed here as a bandage to hold the poultice of 'dust' in place and one might presume, to aid the staunching of blood. Using linen for bandaging features many times in Mildþryþ's remedies.

There are also references to her using linen as a covering for medicinal ingredients, perhaps to keep insects off the preparations and on one occasion there is a directive to burn salt upon linen cloth to help cure 'black blain'. It has been unclear what black blain referred to in the sixth to ninth century as in later years it specified an animal-only disease similar to foot and mouth, but in the next remedy from the *Lacnunga* manuscript, it is identified as a human sickness:

'Gif men eglað seo blace blegen, þonne nime man great sealt, bærne on linenum claðe swa micel swa an æg, grinde þonne þæt sealt smæl, nime þonne þreora ægra, geolcan, swinge hit swiðe togædere ond lege hit vi niht þærto, nim þonne eorðnafelan ond grundeswylian ond cawelleaf ond eald smera, cnuca þæt eal tosomne ond lege hit þreo niht þærto, nim þonne gearwan ond grundewylian ond bræmbelleaf ond clæne spic, cnuca togædere ond lege þærto, him bið sona sel, oððæt hit hal s yond ne cume þær æt nan wæta, butan of þan wyrtan sylfan.'

'If the black blain ails a man, then coarse salt shall be taken, burn it on linen cloth, as much as an egg, then grind the salt very small, then take three eggs' yolks, whip it strongly together and lay it on for six nights, then take earthnavel and groundsel, and cabbage leaf, and old fat, pound it together and lay it on for three nights, then take yarrow and groundsel and bramble leaf and clean bacon,

pound them together and lay them on, it shall soon be better for
him, yet until he is healthy, let no water come to him except from
the herbs themselves.'

Mildþryþ's world comes alive within this remedy for black blain. She relays to the person collecting these remedies exactly how she would go about curing the illness – what herbal ingredients she recommends, how to prepare them and how long it will take for the procedure to work. This isn't a quick prescription. A total of nine nights is required for this cure along with three different concoctions, and it is probable that this is not the end of the treatment.

Within the *Lacnunga* are two further remedies for black blain, each with slightly different characteristics such as a further poultice and a ritualistic chant. When viewed alongside the above cure, what emerges is a lengthy, involved but coherent and sophisticated remedy. It is therefore possible to suggest that the scribes fragmented one original complex cure into three parts.

In the second part of the cure we are told that if a 'black blain' boil is particularly swollen it must be 'opened up' and then covered with a poultice of salt and sticky yolk. This poultice is to be bound with linen, and binding salt to a boil or abscess is something we continue to do today to draw out the infection. Although something of an old wives' tale, salt is nonetheless absorbent and has anti-bacterial properties.

The third part of the cure for black blain brings in a ritualistic element that involves chanting over the boils:

'Bind, bind, bind, calicet aclu cluel sedes adclocles acre earcre
arnem nonabiuð ær ærnem niðren arcum cunað arcum arctua
fligara uglen binchi cutern nicparam raf afð egal uflen arta arta
arta trauncula trauncula.'

The chant, beginning with the words 'bind, bind, bind' might have been sung whilst the boils were being bound with the linen bandage. This chant has defied translation and possibly consists of now forgotten words, or alternatively, it could be a purposively paradoxical element similar to what we might understand today as speaking in tongues. Following the chant is a prayer or spell that states the healer's intention for the boils to 'dry up' and 'grow no larger'.

The descriptions of black boils in the three remedies are vivid enough to support a theory that black blain, in the sixth century, referred to what we term the plague or Black Death. Although it is generally accepted that the

Black Death did not reach Britain until the fourteenth century, some ancient sources do point to a flourish of it occurring in the sixth century.

The plague of Justinian was bubonic plague and this epidemic killed twenty-five million people in the Roman Empire between 541-542. It had reached Ireland by 544 and there is speculative evidence within a report of the death of the Welsh King Maelgwn Gwynedd in 547, that he died of plague. Yet scholars generally contend that no evidence exists to believe that plague reached what we today term England during this time, although it has been suggested that the Roman town of Calleva (Silchester in Hampshire) fell due to the plague of Justinian.

The abandonment of smaller Roman towns during the Anglo-Saxon period was not unusual however. Yet if the plague did reach England in the sixth century, then we would expect to find remedies for it in the Mildþryþ's Old English healing books, especially as Calleva was in the centre of Hwicce country, close to neighbouring Wales where King Maelgwn Gwynedd died. 'Black blain' might therefore, be the missing evidence proving the Black Death occurred in England before the fourteenth century.

Black Blain obviously required medical care far beyond the requirement of a modest boil and so here we may have, surviving unnoticed in the Old English texts, the most complete and sophisticated ancient indigenous remedy for the Black Death that exists. That it was recorded in Hwicce country lends support for the theory that *Bald's Leechbook III* and *Lacnunga* were indeed sourced from sixth century materials as this was the time when the plague would have been present and in the very time and place where Mildþryþ and her descendants were working.

By viewing the activities of Mildþryþ's career and the grave goods placed with her upon death, a vivid picture is beginning to emerge. The encounter with black blain exposes her abilities and relationships, demonstrating the manner of her medical role. William Bynam has separated the history of medicine into five general chronological categories. He states these to be 'bedside, library, hospital, community and laboratory' and that these 'represent the different roles of doctors, as well as reflecting the differing sites in which they work.' Mildþryþ can be seen in the remedy for black blain in a particularly 'bedside' category of healthcare, as might be expected for the time, and we can only imagine the scene which may have unfolded when the ancient occupants of Bidford-on-Avon first encountered the plague:

Fear would have been as palpable as the stench of death when plague came to the villages and towns of Hwicce country. The best physicians would have been called to treat this unknown visitor that mercilessly putrefied the internal organs of its host whilst bulging from the skin in large black necrotic bleeding pustules. From the moment Mildþryþ entered the patient's dwelling, she would have been taking in the scene with its variety of smells, the voices of worried family and the fearful, pain-ridden figure of the patient, around whom a certain chaos might well have been present.

In a cure that spans a number of days, a positive, nurturing bedside manner would have been important. Also, a degree of authoritative persona and diplomatic social engagement would have been essential as Mildþryþ commandeered the family hearth, brewed the tonics and created poultices. Family members might have been called on to find the more unusual elements of the cure, perhaps those not carried in Mildþryþ's daily 'doctor's bag'. The egg yolk would need to be fresh and bacon might need to be bought. Neighbours and friends, worried but fearful for their own families might flurry about, seeking information, wanting to know what is wrong – 'What's the matter with him?' someone might ask, 'do we need to be concerned? Tell us what we should do.'

Mildþryþ, along with many of her colleagues, was young, perhaps just turning twenty when faced with a disease so terrible that little precedent existed except the immediate treatment of observable symptoms such as the lancing and cleaning of the boils and soothing compresses for swollen lymph glands. Today we know that this would have done nothing to halt the plague, and Mildþryþ may have realised this quickly as she turned to further, more supernatural alternatives when the poultices failed.

When six nights of egg and salt did little to halt the sickness, Mildþryþ then tried three nights of herbs. Earthnavel was used to cure ulcers and groundsel has a long history of use within poultices for wounds and skin conditions. Dioscorides says of it, 'The people in Lincolnshire use this externally against pains and swelling, and as they affirm with great success.' Cabbage leaves relieve swelling and pain. Mildþryþ's treatment would have worked well had these skin eruptions been isolated from the underlying condition of plague.

With all eyes upon her, Mildþryþ does all she can to cure the incurable. With pharmacology failing, even with the added authority of divine Trinitarian intervention invoked by the direction of 'six nights', then 'three nights', there is just one thing left to try – magic. So, she begins to chant, '*Bind, bind, bind, calicet aclu cluel sedes adclocles acre earcre arnem nonabiuð ær ærnem niðren arcum...*'

This type of chant is termed the *voces magicae* or magical voice by the Oxford professor of medieval languages Alderik Blom. He explains how these mantras were used to identify a specific moment of transformation where the ritualistic language symbolises a connection with the supernatural or divine. It is purposely ambiguous and characteristic of shamanic language, where literal meaning is obscured in a spirit dialect. Within a healing ritual, this would create an atmosphere of a deeply meaningful and experiential nature. We find the *voces magicae* being used in a number of Mildþryþ's remedies:

'Wið ðon þe mon oððe nyten wyrm gedrince gyf hyt sy wæpnedcynnes sing ðis leoð in þæt swiðre eare þe her æfter awriten is, gif hit sy wifcynnes sing in þæt wynstre eare, Gonomil orgomil marbumil marbsai ramun tofeð tengo docuillo biran cuiðær cæfmiil scuiht cuillo scuiht cuib duill marbsiramum. Sing nygon siðan in þæt eare þis galdor ond pater noster æne.'

'In case a man or beast should drink a worm, if it be of male gender sing this song, that is written below, into the right ear, if be of the female gender sing it into the left ear. Gonomil orgomil marbumil marbsai ramun tofeð tengo docuillo biran cuiðær cæfmiil scuiht cuillo scuiht cuib duill marbsiramum. Sing this nine times into the ear and 'pater noster' once.'

In this cure for worms, the chant is to be sung into the ear. Similarly to the previous remedy, the words *Gonomil orgomil marbumil marbsai ramun tofeð tengo docuillo biran cuiðær cæfmiil scuiht cuillo scuiht cuib duill marbsiramum* have never been adequately translated. Most theorists believe them nonsensical, akin to the shamanic language of the magical voice. Yet in this case it has been posited that the first words at least, might be Old Irish and could be translated as, 'I slay the beast, I slaughter the beast, I kill the beast.' This formula would certainly make sense in relation to the 'slaying' of the troublesome worm. Also, Old Irish features a number of times in Mildþryþ's *books*.

A further suggestion might be that the words *cuiðær, cuillo, and cuib* refer to the ancient goddess Cuda or Cuðær who was worshipped in the sixth century in the region where Mildþryþ lived. During this time Cuðær was the Hwicce's goddess and her image can be found on a number of stone reliefs accompanied by three male escorts standing before a large cauldron. It may be that Mildþryþ and her fellow physicians drew upon ancient Irish magic to encourage their goddess to intervene in a cure for worms.

Although the Christian scribes and those collecting these cures for the monastery tried wherever they could, to alter and Christianise the earlier pagan content, it is perhaps a quirk of fate that the name of Mildþryþ's goddess, the goddess of the Hwicce, might have gone unnoticed here, hidden among the seemingly nonsensical. The use of the magical voice features in a number of later witch trials involving cunning-women. The accused witch Girolama del Cocó for example, had a reputation for successful healing and as Lizanne Kallestrup describes:

'All the witnesses took for granted that the rituals were working … witnesses emphasized that the ritual involved a prayer combined with reciting incomprehensible words or mumbling. The effect was certainly welcome but the incomprehensible words and mumblings in the rituals were what made the witnesses denounce Girolama.'

Chapter 4

Magically Empowered

Had herbal healing been the only activity employed by Mildþryþ to assist her community, then history may have been kinder. Yet she lived during a time when natural science blended with the metaphysical and this interdependent meeting of natural and supernatural worlds meant that causality was not always seen as a matter of cognitive problem solving in relation to observable facts. Other, less obvious reasons for illness were often involved, such as the unwanted attention of mischievous elves or a mistaken insult to a local deity. When cause was determined to be supernatural in origin, then magic was the supernatural tool of choice.

For example, Mildþryþ's bucket pendants, twelve in all, contained an unusually large amount of thread. Bucket pendants are literally as they sound – small pendants shaped like tiny buckets. Often, they have been found to contain remnants of fat and herbs indicating a magical aspect to healing – the Warwickshire research team says of them that they 'are believed to have had symbolic and magical purpose'. It has been suggested that bucket pendants came to Britain with the Saxons and although the pendants have been discovered as early as the first century during the Roman occupation, they are extremely rare, and most are discovered within the migration patterns of the Germanic tribes. Some researchers contend that the tradition originated in Southern Russia.

These pendants are almost exclusively discovered within female graves with cunning-woman associations and although some suggest that the herbs and fats contained within the pendants might have offered some pharmaceutical benefit when the substances evaporated, the large quantities of non-organic materials point to a supernatural interpretation; in Himlingøje, Denmark, a woman was buried with her bucket pendants stored in a stunning silver amulet box. Where the pendants are found accompanying ordinary individuals, then the magical healing significance becomes apparent from their placement. In Gródek am Bug, Poland for example, a skeleton was unearthed with 'bucket pendants on the right knee, left elbow, left lower rib and right shoulder, and each location showed a healed fracture'. Mildþryþ's pendants contained large quantities of thread rather than organic matter alone and as researcher Jill Smith explains, there was a particular fondness for using thread in magical rituals:

'The "charms of the threads" or "*eolas an t-snaithein*" involved the use of red, white and black threads which represented the eclipsed moon, the full moon and the dark moon. These were entwined about the affected part and an incantation muttered over the patient three times. There are still people practicing this traditional and ancient form of healing, but they are hard to find. There is/was also the "barr a'chian" – the "top of the head", which involves winding red threads round the neck while reciting a charm to drive evil spirits out through the top of the head.'

The *eolas an t-snaithein* is a Celtic ritual and Jill Smith has found that the Celts used red thread abundantly in their healing ceremonies. Mildþryþ may therefore have been drawing upon Celtic magic by her use of amuletic thread. We know from her grave that she was a pagan Saxon, who nonetheless wore the dualistic propaganda of Celtic and Saxon motifs upon her person. As a physician, this impartiality may have served her community similarly to our General Practitioners today, most of whom set aside their personal opinions regarding politics and religion so as not to isolate any member of their community who comes forward in need.

Thread magic was not unknown to the Saxons but the particular use of red thread, often combined with rowan wood, was a Celtic tradition for healing and protection. The rowan and thread was associated with the sainted Celtic goddess Brighid, whose pagan rites survive today in the corn-dollies and solar crosses made by Christians and pagans alike at harvest time. Both symbols were used as amulets to ward off evil and invite the great goddess's protection.

Belief in the sanctity of the rowan tree prevailed well into the conversion times as folklorist James Napier explains:

'It could also be shown that tree worship has been combined with Christianity. The rowan tree was held sacred by the Druids, and is often found among their stone monuments ... and when these nations were converted to Christianity, they did not fall away from their belief in the sanctity of the rowan tree.'

Mildþryþ certainly used red thread in her healing repertoire. In her Old English herbals for example, we find it being used in a remedy where the roots of plantain (waybread) are to be tied around the patient's head to cure a headache:

'Adelf wegbrædan butan isene ær sunnan upgange, bind þa moran ymb þæt heafod mid wræte reade þræde, sona him bið sel.'

'Dig waybread without iron and before the sun rises, bind the roots around the head with a red thread, it will soon be better for him.'

This remedy contains a number of magical formulae. First, we are told to dig up waybread without using iron tools. This directive supports the theory that remedies such as this are very old and possibly pre-date the Iron Age. Although iron would become a metal with its own magical importance, at first it was viewed similarly to most new-fangled things – with suspicion, hence the recommendation to avoid its use.

In his book *Anglo-Saxon Magic* (1948), Godfrid Storms suggests the phrase 'Dig it up without iron', which is found in a number of the remedies, may act as a reminder to the healer to use another magical tool instead, such as a sword – and swords are certainly used within some of the more ritualistic cures. Unfortunately, of course, swords during this era were made of iron, yet Storms may nonetheless be correct if indeed these particular cures pre-date the sixth century. Perhaps the magical tool was a sword made of bronze.

Next, we are directed to a certain time of the day – the time just before the sun rises. Symbolically, this marks the revelation of that which was once hidden in darkness and these changes from dark to light were considered extremely auspicious moments of supernatural power.

The ritualistic use of red thread, wrapped around the head, has been identified as far across Europe as the Celtic culture spread. With new archaeological evidence proving that the Celts inhabited vaster swathes of the continent than previously believed, Carlo Ginzburg has found remnants of their ritualistic beliefs in the Mediterranean. Whilst investigating the shamanistic origins of witchcraft, Ginzburg uncovered an unusual Italian tradition of magically empowered women using red thread to heal.

In the Friuli district of North Eastern Italy, a unique class of visionary women called 'good-walkers' (*benandanti)* were said to protect the local communities against evil sorcerers (*streghe*). Ginzburg's research revealed that these good-walkers were divinely chosen for this important task due to a curious birth anomaly; the goddess marked them at birth by delivering them into the world along with an intact umbilical sac with the bloodied cord wrapped about the baby's head like a large red thread. This winding of red cord about the head became a powerful symbolic marker of medico-magical power and such babies were believed to be chosen healers, representing the divine on Earth. By tying red thread around a patient's head during healing rituals, this divine authority was symbolically invoked to drive out the spirit causing the illness or headache.

Those chosen by the goddess to be good-walkers were blessed with further divine gifts. Although medicine was their main virtue along with abilities of prophecy and magic, they also served as priestesses and spiritual warriors – roles and abilities that Ginzburg and others term 'shamanic'.

In their role as spiritual warrior, they waged war against the *streghe*. Night-time battles were fought for the wellbeing of the local people. By the light of the moon, each side would take position in the spring fields before the crops were sown. The good-walkers would fight for the health and wealth of the community and its crops whilst the sorcerers would be battling for their demise. The outcome of this nocturnal battle would determine the fortunes of local people for the coming year.

This character of righteous warring recalls the Nordic Valkyries. Although well known to us today as warrior women responsible for choosing the dead for Valhalla, their earlier character was more nuanced with emblems of them appearing in Old English literature and Church documents. In the eleventh century for example, the English Bishop Wulfstan states in his homilies that the Valkyries were '*wicce* sinners and evil-doers'. By this time therefore, it was not just Mildþryþ and her kind being branded as witches. The term was gradually expanding its claim towards any woman, real or mythic who embodied magical powers, and the Valkyrie were no exception.

From Old English literature, Jennifer Culver has discovered that the early figure of the Valkyrie bears characteristic similarities with the role of British cunning-women. Hidden within poems such as *The Wife's Lament* and *Wulf and Eadwacer* from the *Exeter Book,* Culver is revealing an earlier, more nuanced face of the Valkyrie. This Anglicised version was known as the *mihtigan wif* (mighty wife) who 'could fight and defend as well as nurture and weave peace'. The *mihtigan wif,* along with the cunning-women and good-walkers, are all female identities that include the attributes of magic, healing, strength and just judgment, hinting at a possibly unified, ancient and complex feminine archetype that embodied characteristics of both benevolence and strength – a contested persona that might well have evoked both respect and fear in the hearts of the community. A poem from the *Exeter Book* describes a Valkyrie before the figure became equated with '*wicce* sinners and evil-doers':

> 'Biþ sio modder mægene eacen, wundrum bewreþed, wistum gehladen, hordum gehroden, hæleþum dyre. Mægen biδ gemiclad, meaht gesweotlad, wlite biþ geweorþad wuldornyttingum. Wynsum wuldorgimm wloncum getenge clægeorn biδ ond cystig cræft eacen; hio biþ eadgum leof, earmum getæse, freolic, sellic.'

> *'She is mother to mighty power, wonderfully supported, food loaded, hoards adorned, dear to heroes. Strength is increased, might manifested, beautiful is honored by wondrous things. A delightful glorious sun orb adorns her generously, yearning after purity and bountiful, she is mighty in skill; She is dear to happy, useful to the miserable, free, strange.'*

A further link between the British cunning-women and the Valkyrie is seen symbolically. There are images dating back to the seventh century depicting Valkyries as cup-bearers, the cup being symbolic of their associations with water, abundance and with their specific protection of swans, who are beautiful yet fierce. Similarly, Stephen Yeates has identified the cup as being the symbol of the Hwicce's personal goddess Cuδær. Yeates postulates that the word Hwicce actually translates as 'sacred vessel' and so the very name of the tribe emerges from their central goddess. Cuδær is indeed pictured in a number of reliefs with her cauldron or cup.

Yeates describes in his book *The Tribe of Witches* (2008) that:

> 'Their name (Hwicce) is one of the most unusual of tribal names in Britain recorded at that date, as the word which is of an Old English origin has been interpreted as meaning Sacred Vessel. This word is directly associated with the Old English word *wicce*, a female participant of witchcraft, which provides the origins for the modern word witch. This means that the tribe was only one of two in Britain which potentially had a name directly associated with pre-Christian religion.'

The *hw* of the word *hwicce* is a Germanic linguistic formula reduced from the *gw* prefix and it should be noted that *Gewisse* referred to the first Saxon settlers of Britain. *Gewisse* translates as 'the educated (wise) ones' and it is likely that the Hwicce took their name from this early migration with *Gewisse* evolving into the term *Hwicce*. Yet Andrew Reynolds maintains this is still far from satisfactory stating:

> 'That the kingdom of the Hwicce does not follow the same naming pattern as other major territories in the west is a matter of interest and may reflect an as yet unidentified difference in its origins compared to its neighbours.'

Richard Coates also suggests that the name is not Saxon but rather, comes from the ancient Celtic *Hǽwïkk* meaning 'the most excellent ones'.

Ginzburg's investigations into the good-walkers of Italy is presented in his 1992 book *The Night Battles* and confirms a widespread European belief in a benevolent class of divinely authorised women using sacred magic to assist the needs of humanity. He also confirms that this belief existed well into the witch trial period.

Within trial transcripts from the area, he discovered many good-walkers caught up in the witch-hunt hysteria. They were evident from motifs of healing, visionary quests and a desire to battle evil. When Christianity became dominant they had been happy to align themselves with it, fighting with Christ against Satan and evildoers. Yet their supernatural beliefs, specifically that they were chosen and divinely authorised, made them a target for the Inquisition despite their Christian conversion.

Ginzburg concluded that the good-walkers were part of a widespread fertility cult that reached from the Northern territories to Central Southern Europe. Although engaged in beneficial activities, their beliefs attracted the attention of the Inquisition who could simply see no difference between their good practices and the evil of their adversaries. Therefore, just as Mildþryþ and the British cunning-women would become assimilated into the category of black magic sorcerers in Northern Europe, the *benandanti* were similarly demonised as being the same as the *streghe*.

The status and role of such women in pre-Christian Europe and Scandinavia did not sit comfortably with the incoming religion, where power, both supernatural and worldly, was under the auspices of men alone. Although in Anglo-Saxon society those who held political power were predominantly male, women had not been without representation. For example, *Æthelflæd*, daughter of Alfred the Great ruled Mercia in the ninth century and was succeeded by her daughter *Ælfwynn*. Angus Wainwright comments regarding *Æthelflæd's* political role that she:

'played a vital role in England in the first quarter of the tenth century. The success of Edward's campaigns against the Danes depended to a great extent upon her cooperation. In the Midlands and the North she came to dominate the political scene. And the way in which she used her influence helped to make possible the unification of England under kings of the West Saxon royal house. But her reputation has suffered from bad publicity, or rather from a conspiracy of silence among her West Saxon contemporaries.'

The 'conspiracy of silence' is an interesting aside as it indicates that her political power was not entirely welcome. By the tenth century, the view of women in society had already started to change, although they were still afforded numerous benefits and rights that were to be absent by the time of Queen Victoria. For example, they were allowed to divorce their husbands, and from early documents it is also evident that women owned much of the household goods and were entitled to equal shares of property.

Mildþryþ might not have commanded political authority, but as a cunning-woman she certainly held an esteemed place in her community as is attested by her grave goods. Memory of her benevolence and power can also be discerned from poetry and charms used by common folk in their times of need as this Old English charm to prevent bees from swarming describes:

'Against a swarm of bees take earth, cast it with your right hand
and under your right foot, saying-
I seize it underfoot, I've found it now:
Lo! Earth has might over all creatures,
And against malice, and over mindlessness,
And over humanity with its greedy tongue.
Throw light soil over them as they swarm, saying-
Sit, cunning women, settle on earth:
never to the woodland flying wild.
Please be mindful of my fortune
as all men are of food and home.'

Here, cunning-women are themselves being invoked to assist with beekeeping. Beekeeping is an ancient tradition. The historian Malcolm Fraser detailed a meticulous history of beekeeping in Britain and found evidence that for the ancient Britons, 'beekeeping in wicker hives had been practiced from time immemorial'. The tradition certainly continued throughout the Anglo-Saxon era and into the modern day.

The Anglo-Saxons believed that bees were highly intelligent. Through observation, they saw an efficient community where food was stored and cooperation provided for future security. They also believed that bees had a connection to the supernatural world and could foretell the weather. More than this, however, they believed that bees connected the world of the living to the realm of the dead.

A curious custom found predominantly in Britain is known as the 'telling of the bees'. The folklorist Samuel Drake recounts how the bees should always be informed of a family member's death by hanging black drapes upon the hive whilst singing a sad tune. If this respect is not paid to the hive and the bees duly informed, then they will fly away. Similarly, if a marriage is to take place in the family the bees should be included in the festivities by decorating their hive with wedding garb.

In this Old English charm for a swarm of bees (*wiþ ymbe),* the beekeeper is acknowledging the superiority of nature over the knowledge of men. Using dirt to encourage the bees to desist from swarming he then continues to liken them, sympathetically, to cunning-women like Mildþryþ, who are viewed as equally knowledgeable and sacred as his beloved bees.

Chapter 5

Riddle me This

*'And farder declarit, That mony folkis in the countre came to hir
to get witt of geir stollin fra thame.'*

'And it is further declared, that many people in the country came
to her to find that which was stolen from them.'
Robert Pitcairn, *Ancient Criminal Trials in Scotland*, 1833.

With her foot planted in both the natural and supernatural worlds, Mildþryþ
was called upon to assist in more than just healthcare. Sickness was not the
only cause of suffering which required her intervention; further issues such
as theft and violence were equally troublesome and similarly to illness,
were viewed as part of a wider landscape of unseen forces. These forces or
energies permeated all life, at every level. The physical world might have
been tough and unyielding, but it could also be a place of enchantment
and magic where, 'A prayer could be answered. A spell could cure. A look
could kill.'

In sixth century Bidford-on-Avon, theft, even of something as mundane
as clothes or kitchen utensils, could impact a family greatly. Victims would
often have to remake the lost items or buy them again at considerable
expense. A serious theft, such as a cow, could devastate a family and be the
difference between eating and starvation. Livestock were of great value to
the people of early Britain – from peasants to landowners, cattle, pigs and
sheep were important revenue and any ill that befell them had a number of
negative consequences.

In Mildþryþ's day, the Hwicce communities and those throughout
Britain, worked upon a principle of folk-right, a type of common law that
emerged as an expression of the moral and judicial consciousness of the
local community. In a time before even the shires, moots and witan existed to
deal with criminal offences, common folk were vulnerable to the actions of
unscrupulous individuals. There was little hope of any help or intervention

for poor folk when things went wrong and with no insurance against theft, many turned to the one person who could provide help – Mildþryþ.

Protection against larceny and charms to locate thieves pepper the Old English books of remedies, and probably formed a large part of Mildþryþ's work as this charm against theft illustrates:

'Garmund, godes ðegen, find þæt feoh and fere þæt feoh and hafa þæt eoh and heald þæt feoh and fere ham þæt feoh.

'þæt he næfre næbbe landes, þæt he hit oðlæde, ne foldan, þæt hit oðferie, ne husa, þæt he hit oðhealde.

'Gif hyt hwa gedo, ne gedige hit him næfre!

'Binnan þrym nihtum cunne ic his mihta, his mægen and his mihta and his mundcræftas.

'Eall he weornige, swa syre wudu weornie, swa breðel seo swa þystel, se ðe ðis feoh oðfergean þence oððe ðis orf oðehtian ðence.'

'Garmund, servant of God, find me those cattle and fetch me those cattle, and have those cattle, and hold those cattle, and bring those cattle home. So he never has land where he can lead them, or ground to bring them to, or a house to keep them in.

'If one do this deed, let it never benefit him!

'Within three nights I will know his might, his strength and his might and his protective crafts.

'May he wither entirely, like wood withered by fire. Be as brittle as a thistle, he who thinks to thieve these cattle or carry off these cows.'

This Old English charm, translated by Gavin Chappell, is representative of a metric, poetic song. Here the identity Garmund is invoked to assist the cunning-woman in locating lost cattle and ensuring that the person responsible for stealing them, or any person hence, will not succeed in their intent, as 'he never has land where he can lead them'. Further, that they will suffer consequences of being diminished similarly to 'wood withered by fire'.

The plentiful examples of this type of criminal intervention within Mildþryþ's repertoire of remedies demonstrate an aspect to ancient folk-right that has been unexplored: here we can see that cunning-women acted in an investigatory and judiciary manner. Also, they acted preventively, conjuring a deterrent against future crimes and perhaps even embodying, by way of

35

their status and supernatural abilities, a further deterrent such as we have today in our police force.

This charm against theft is a basic legal formulation or folk-right in action; the cunning-woman acts to locate the lost property and then to ensure the criminal is not successful and will be exposed as she seeks to 'know his might' and his 'protective crafts'. Then finally, justice is served as the perpetrator becomes as 'brittle as a thistle'. Although the methodology reflects the cosmology of the time and is therefore, supernatural, the process and intention is nonetheless familiar.

Of particular interest here is the name Garmund. *Wermund* is the Germanic form of *Germund* and he is mentioned in Beowulf as *Garmundes*, a skilled fighter and father of Offa the Angle. King Offa, who ruled Hwicce country from 757 until his death in 796, was of Anglo-Saxon royalty and descended, according to pagan belief, from the god Woden. There is even a folk tale that the earlier pagan King Penda who ruled Hwicce country from 626 to 656, used names to surreptitiously continue his pagan beliefs into the Christian era and so incorporated the name Woden into what is now Warwick, as tribute to his illustrious ancestor.

The *Anglo-Saxon Chronicle* entry for 755 AD says of King Offa that he:

> 'was the son of Thingferth, Thingferth of Enwulf, Enwulf of Osmod, Osmod of Eawa, Eawa of Webba, Webba of Creoda, Creoda of Cenwald, Cenwald of Cnebba, Cnebba of Icel, Icel of Eomer, Eomer of Angelthew, Angelthew of Offa, Offa of Wermund, Wermund of Witley, Witley of Woden.'

It seems Garmund, of the lineage of Woden was held as a protective symbol by the Anglo-Saxons, someone who when called upon could intervene to offer assistance, rather as some might call upon the intervention of Saints or the archangel Michael today.

In the British Museum there is a ninth century gold ring with the inscription, '*GARMUND MEC AH IM*'. The words *mec ah* are a common device of ownership from Anglo-Saxon times, so translated it reads 'Garmund owns me.' It is unknown whether the name refers to the personal possessor, or whether it was used to invoke the protection of the noble Garmund, descendent of Woden. In this case, it is most likely to be the former, as self-referential inscriptions of this type were common formulae of ownership.

Objects, especially jewellery and weapons, were important symbols of wealth and status. By marking such an item with a motif of ownership, the person was affirming their own importance as a possessor of the object, which was often beautiful and well crafted. A silver brooch found in Leicestershire makes this clear stating *Wulfgyfe me ah ag hire* (Wulfgyfe owns me for herself). Wulgyfe is not taking any chances, dissatisfied with the usual *me ah* formula she adds *ag hire*. Wulfgyfe was not sharing her brooch with anyone.

Another lady taking no chances with her brooch lived in nearby Cambridgeshire. Her inscription reads: *Ædwen me ag age hyo drihten drihten hine awerie þe me hire æfterie buton hyo me selle hire agenes willes* (Ædwen owns me, may the Lord own her, may the Lord curse him who takes me from her, unless she give me of her own free will). Sean Mock (2016) explains how *Ædwen* is likening her ownership to that of God's and that 'the brooch can name a chain of ownership and threaten would-be criminals,' thereby demonstrating her personal power, agency and the divine lineage of that power.

Mildþryþ's methods for retrieving stolen items and protecting against further thefts are apparent from her remedies, yet other means of locating stolen goods are evident from objects accompanying cunning-woman burials. For example, a number of women were interred with items related to divination; a number of crystal balls have been found, yet where their utility remains quite obvious to us today, less familiar are the sieves and shears.

Although Mildþryþ was not buried with crystal balls, sieves or shears, many of her colleagues were. Often placed between a cunning-woman's knees, crystal balls have been found dating from the early fifth century, although most are from the South East of England and dwindle quickly with the rise of Christianity. A Saxon import it seems, that did not survive long enough to migrate far west. A particularly fine example from Dover, Kent, dates to the sixth century and is contained within an ornate silver frame and archaeologists believe it was worn, hanging from the woman's waist like the 'doctor's bag'.

Similarly, perforated spoons which are often elaborately decorated with engraving and precious stones, also hung from the waist. These are refined, carefully made objects and along with Mildþryþ's artisanal long handled scalpel, become tokens of identity. Conspicuously worn, they mark out specific individuals within an increasingly complex society. Cunning-women from the sixth century did not hide themselves away in woodland hovels;

their role and abilities were embodied and socially advertised by costumes, just as judges, doctors and law enforcement are today.

Eight instances of crystal balls have been discovered along with the sieve type spoons and shears, and come almost extensively from early pre-Christian Saxon burials. One history website depicting such finds asks, 'Why does this spoon have holes in it?' and 'What was this mysterious crystal ball used for? Answers on a postcard.'

The use of the sieve spoons is contested. Some researchers argue they were for sieving wine whilst others counter that the holes are too big to sustain the theory and instead they were used for prophylactic sprinkling. Prophylactic sprinkling, whereby an area is cleansed by sprinkling water imbued with herbs, could explain a large-holed sieve. Sprinkling is a rare directive however, and from current research only appears in a medical codex written by the Syrian physician Qusta ibn Luqa in the ninth century as a recommendation for travellers on their way to Mecca. To protect the pilgrim from vermin he recommends that one should:

> 'sprinkle one's habitat where one is not secure from vermin with water in which has been cooked chamomile, colocynth, harmel or garlic...'

Colin Mackenzie in *Five Thousand Receipts*, 1829, says that one should, 'sprinkle bay leaves, or worm-wood, or lavender, or walnut leaves...' to drive away caterpillars, although no sieve is mentioned or required.

Sieves were certainly used by Mildþryþ in her region of Britain as we find reference to them in her healing books. In a remedy for cardiacus (which the author has identified to be English Sweating Sickness) there is a directive to 'sift barley meal' (*beren meala gesyft*) as part of the ingredients for a poultice. Yet sifting fine meal and powders seems incongruous with the large sized holes of the mysterious perforated spoons. Although a sieve of some sort may have formed part of Mildþryþ's general doctor's kit, being used to sift ingredients to form powders, there is a further use to be considered for the large-holed spoons. When viewed contextually along with the shears, another possibility begins to emerge.

The cunning-woman from Westbury-by-Shenley, a village situated east of Bidford-on-Avon, was discovered with a pair of shears. Similarly to Mildþryþ, she is young and the shears along with a knife were contained within the now iconic 'doctor's bag', and as Andrew Reynolds acknowledges she 'is evidently of special character'. So, what were cunning-women actually doing with these odd large-holed sieve spoons and shears? Fortunately, the strange use to which they have for centuries been put was recorded at many points during the Middle Ages and into the Early Modern Period. For example, the philosopher John Aubrey collected ancient customs from Wiltshire, in the heart of ancient Hwicce territory and stated in 1686 that:

> 'The Sheers are stuck in a Sieve, and two maydens hold up ye sieve with the top of their fingers by the handle of the shiers: then say, By St Peter & St Paule such a one hath stoln (such a thing), the others say, By St Peter and St Paul he hath not stoln it. After many such Adjurations, the Sieve will turne at ye name of ye Thiefe.'

The sieve and shears are being used here to reveal the identity of a thief. Today this form of divination is known as coscinomancy and although the word is Greek in origin, the custom probably had its Anglo-Saxon equivalent term that has been lost. In the Middle Ages, the practice was known as 'turning the riddle' or simply 'the sieve and shears'. Riddle comes from the Old English *hridder*, which evolved into *hriddel* before losing its Germanic '*h*' prefix and becoming our modern word riddle. Gardeners are familiar with the riddle, as it is a tool used to sieve stones from compost.

In Aubrey's recording of the above event of riddle turning, there is a clear indication that women, 'two maydens', must lead the ritual and hold the sieve and shears before using 'adjurations' to discern the thief.

An earlier report from 1382 finds the practice used in the now lost parish of St Mildred, Poultry in London. This time, it seems the correct tools were not to hand and a gentleman named Robert Berewold, perhaps having seen the ritual performed elsewhere, improvised, as the following account describes.

A bowl had been stolen from Robert's house and he wanted to find the culprit and seek justice. To this end, he constructed an approximation of the sieve and shears to divine the name of the thief. The records describe how he used a loaf of bread as a riddle supported by four knives and a wooden peg in place of the shears. The loaf would move and turn in response to the names he stated until, we may assume, it moved in a conspicuous way when he uttered the name 'Johanna Wolsy'. When Robert made his formal accusation against Johanna, however, in this instance his method of divination was not appreciated and he was duly accused of 'maliciously lying'.

Riddle turning continued well into the sixteenth century as a way of locating stolen goods. In 1586 for example, Tibbie Smart from the tiny Aberdeenshire village of Mickle Coull went on trial for witchcraft. According to witnesses, she was well known for locating lost cattle by means of the shears and riddle. Also, according to one Alexander Gray, she used the contraption for assessing the health of livestock too. Her neighbour Robert Allan had sought her services in this regard and Tibbie foretold that all his sheep and lambs would die that very year, and so they did.

Her accusers described Tibbie as 'ane common and notorious witch'. It was relayed in her trial how John Davidson, 'ane puir man' had discovered a strange bag belonging to Tibbie that contained salt crystals, barley seeds, coal and an array of coloured threads. Davidson had decided to burn the bag but when Tibbie discovered this she went to him in anger and cursed him. Following the curse, Davidson became 'incontinent thaireftir tuik siknes and dwynit on be the space of aught dayis and deceissit' (he took ill with incontinence, wasted away and died after eight days). Unusually, Tibbie was not executed. Instead she was branded upon the cheek and exiled.

As late as 1898 the custom remained strong and is described by Joseph Wright in *The English Dialect Dictionary* in some detail:

> 'The riddle is set on its side, the points of a pair of large scissors being so fixed in it (separate from each other) that the riddle may be suspended by the hold taken of it by the scissors. One handle of the scissors is placed on the finger of one person and the other on that of another. Some words, to the same purpose with the following, are repeated: "By St Paul and St. Peter, did A.B steal my yarn?" or whatever was lost. If the person mentioned be innocent the riddle remains motionless; if guilty, it immediately turns round. The ancient art of divination by riddle and shears- that is, attempting to discover a culprit or lover by holding a sieve in a pair of scissors or shears, muttering some mystic invocation, and watching the trembling, nodding, turning of the sieve as the names of suspected persons are uttered, ...is a mode of divination for the discovery of theft.'

Although the sieve and shears method of divination was Christianised by Aubrey's time with the inclusion in many reports of adjurations to St Peter and St Paul, it would once have contained earlier pagan chants and prayers. The 'muttering' of 'some mystic invocation' mentioned above may have been a remnant of pre-Christian materials such as we find in the *Lacnunga* manuscript, as this next remedy against theft illustrates:

> '*Wið þeofentum luben luben niga efið niga efið fel ceid fel ceid,*
> *delf fel cumer orcggaei ceufor dard giug farig pidig delou delupih.*'

This is an example of Alderik Blom's *voces magicae* and with no further ritualistic elements noted it seems probable that at one time this nonsensical chant accompanied some form of ritualistic event to protect from theft, or expose a thief. We cannot know if this is perhaps the earliest recorded example of a charm for coscinomancy, but it isn't beyond the realm of possibility that these words were ones used in an ancient riddle turning ritual, interpreted by the listeners as mumbles and 'muttering'.

It was not only the protection of livestock from thieves that was of concern to communities; the health of such animals was of equal importance. Remedies designed to defend animals against illness feature widely within Mildþryþ's repertoire of cures. For example, one of Mildþryþ's remedies protects pigs from sudden death:

> 'Wið swina færsteorfan, do a in heora mete, seoð clitan, syle etan, nim eac elehtran, bisceopwyrt ond cassuc, ðefeþorn, hegerifan, haranspicel, sing ofer feower mæssan, drif on fald, hoh ða wyrte on feower healfe ond on þan dore, bærn do recels to, læt yrnan ofer þone rec.'

> '*Against sudden maurain of pigs, put this always in their food, simmer clite, give it to eat, also take lupin, bishopswort and hassock, hawthorn, hedge rive, harespeckle, sing four masses over [the pigs], drive them into the fold, hang the herbs on four sides and on the door, burn them, add incense, let [the pigs] run across the smoke.*'

This Old English cure is designed to protect pigs from *færsteorfan* (murrain), a general word that referred to a number of diseases including foot-and-mouth, rinderpest and other infections leading to death. Of its herbal ingredients, *clite* (cleavers) has been used for many centuries as good 'cure all' tonic. It continues to be prescribed by herbalists today in the treatment of many conditions from skin lesions to kidney and urinary tract infections. As the basis of a preventative tonic, this would be a useful plant. Yet it is the ritualistic elements that make this cure unusual.

Anthropologist Vera Diakonova was fortunate to experience a healing ritual of the Altaian and Tuvinian shaman of Siberia that is similar to Mildþryþ's remedy for pigs. Whilst conducting ethnographic research in the Seventies, Diakonova witnessed a community shaman helping a family that had suffered from particularly ill health over the previous year. The ritual event occurred in July, a time when the shaman and people believed that the natural world was at its energetic height and abundant with power that could be harnessed for healing. The family, together with the shamanic healer, gathered about a larch tree. It was explained to Diakonova that the tree was selected to match the spirit of the healer and so was sympathetically linked in likenesses such as age and appearance.

The ensuing ceremony contained a number of processes; hearths were placed at the cardinal points around the space, and placed upon the hearth-stones were offerings of food for the spirits and gods who would be invoked for their healing aid. Juniper was then lit, along with further herbs at the four quarters and the healer observed the movement of the smoke as it weaved through the circle. If the vapour moved from west to east, then this was good news as it meant the family was free from the ill that had befallen it over the previous year. The ceremony then continued with chanting and invocations for health, and protection from recurrences of sickness.

In Mildþryþ's remedy for the pigs we find remnants of a similar ceremony. The herbs lupin, bishopswort, hassock, hawthorn, hedge rive and harespeckle are to be burnt upon the four sides of the enclosure and also upon the door. Masses, masking the earlier pagan chants are to be sung over the pigs and finally, incense is added to the blend of herbs and Mildþryþ must ensure the pigs run through the smoke. Although nuances of the ceremony are undoubtedly lost or unrecorded, this healing ritual is not dissimilar to the Siberian one.

The shamanic process of burning herbs for ritual protection is known as smudging, and a number of instances of this survive in Mildþryþ's healing books. All are within remedies that have a protective, preventative intention rather than remedial intervention. Smoking herbs was ritualistic and was thought to cleanse the person or animal of negative, malevolent energies or spirits that were, or were intending, to cause harm.

Old English belief that illness was caused by the malevolence of supernatural beings, spirits or energies is often indicated by use of the word 'shot'. Hag-shot and elf-shot feature often in Mildþryþ's remedies to indicate that these darker creatures were involved in the sickness, as this cure for a horse describes:

'Gif hors gescoten sy oððe oþer neat, nim ompran sæd ond scyttisc wex, gesinge maessepreost xii mæssan ofer ond do halig wæter on, ond do þonne on þæt hors, oððe on swa hwylc neat swa hit sie, hafa þe þa wyrta symle mid.'

'If a horse or other animal be [elf] shot, take dock's seeds and Scottish wax, let a mass-priest sing twelve masses over them and put holy water on, and put it on the horse, or whatever animal it may be, have the herbs always with you.'

Part of this cure is lost and dock is the only herb remaining here. Dock is a good blood cleanser and its seeds have been used for skin complaints and boils. Without further preparation though, dock seeds have little medicinal effect and so it is the ritual that takes centre stage. The masses and holy water, although probably taking the place of earlier pagan material serve to bring a protective element to the animal whilst cleansing the horse of any current negative energy. The direction to 'have the herbs always with you' shows the frequency and importance of this type of cure.

From Mildþryþ's sixth century remedies we find a continued, uninterrupted tradition of cunning-women being sought out to heal and protect livestock well into the Early Modern Era. By the sixteenth century for example, when the witch trials were underway and Mildþryþ had been resting in her grave almost 1500 years, Robert Kirk, a seventeenth century folklorist and priest documented the continued belief and experiences in Scotland regarding cunning-women. One account he relates is that cunning-women would use the shoulder blade (*slinneanachd*) of an un-slaughtered sheep to divine the future wellbeing of families and their livestock:

'by looking into the bone they will tel if whoredom be committed in the Ouners house; what money the Master of the sheep had, if any will die out of that house for that moneth, and if anie cattell there will take a Trake (as if planet-struck) called earchall. Then will they prescribe a preservative and prevention.'

Earchall is Scottish Gaelic for a sudden loss of cattle, similar to Mildþryþ's sudden death of pigs, and *Trake* means to be ill or waste away. A number of concerns are evident from this remedy – there is worry for the welfare of sheep and cattle yet unusually, there is a desire by the 'owner' of the property to know whether any 'whoredom' has happened.

In medieval England and Scotland 'whoredom' did not necessarily mean prostitution as we might expect. Indeed, the English theologian Thomas of Chobham explains that 'If someone sells herself in secret, she is not called a whore'. Instead, medieval female conduct literature aimed to establish normative behaviours for women regarding their interests and bodily practices. As Gina Greco explains in *The Good Wife's Guide,*

> 'Conduct books prescribe women's behavior in their homes and spiritual lives, indicating proper aspirations for their futures. Medieval women and men read and read to from these volumes.'

The man of the house, enquiring after whoredom, was probably seeking clarity regarding the general conduct of his women folk.

The use of herbs, charms, amulets and rituals to procure health, wellbeing and protection were understandable during a time when a lack of personal agency within such matters had potentially devastating consequences. A cunning-woman with a reputation for bringing hope to the helpless by acting in conjunction with the supernatural world, would have been providing a valuable community service. Yet as Louise Kallestrup describes and warns in *Agents of Witchcraft in Early Modern Italy and Denmark,*:

> 'Expressing knowledge of whether an illness would pass or not signified that the person had special access to the supernatural, which put the person in a powerful yet fragile position.'

The fragile position Kallestrup speaks of emerges from the view that cunning-women, although revered, respected and required, nonetheless stood at the boundary of two worlds. Like the shaman, Mildþryþ was gifted with natural and supernatural abilities and this marked her out as being different to other people. She was within society yet at the same time, noticeably distanced by her supernatural contributions. Also, during a time when a new religion from the Far East with an exclusively male god served by exclusively male attendants was set on conversion, Mildþryþ's position became fragile indeed. By the ninth century for example, Halitgar of Cambrai's Roman Penitential would state, 'If anyone makes amulets, which is a detestable thing, he shall do penance for three years.'

Chapter 6

Women only

'Women have always been healers. They were the unlicensed doctors and anatomists of western history. They were abortionists, nurses and counsellors. They were pharmacists, cultivating healing herbs and exchanging the secrets of their uses. They were midwives, travelling from home to home and village to village. For centuries women were doctors without degrees, barred from books and lectures, learning from each other, and passing on experience from neighbor to neighbor and mother to daughter. They were called "wise women" by the people, witches or charlatans by the authorities.'

Witches, Midwives, and Nurses: A History of Women Healers, Barbara Ehrenreich and Deirdre English, 1973.

An intriguing suggestion emerging from British archaeology is that the role of physician in ancient times was not just a female one – it was exclusively women only. Mildþryþ's 'doctor's bag' and other magico-medical items are simply not discovered in the graves of men. Also, it has been observed that within each community graveyard there is but one healer present. This may indicate that cunning-women were not just random followers of an ambiguous healing tradition where herbs and rituals were used by happenstance but rather, were part of a systemised order of exclusively female community physicians.

Yet this idea of exclusivity sits awkwardly within the modern mind. After all, we have all heard of the great physician Hippocrates who practiced in the fifth century BC and Galen in the second century AD. Could Britain have had a uniquely different approach to medicine and healthcare administered by women only? Mildþryþ's Old English healing books of *Lacnunga* and *Bald's Leechbook III* have been clearly identified as being particularly British with few Mediterranean influences. So perhaps it is possible that in Britain, an altogether different, female healthcare system was indeed present.

Archaeology together with the folkloric work of Snorri Sturluson reveals that British cunning-women may have been part of a tradition of female physicians that once existed throughout Britain and Scandinavia. For example, a Danish ring fort near Fyrkat dating from the ninth century contained a particularly striking grave. Similarly to Mildþryþ, the woman it contained was found with a bag filled with amulets and organic matter including henbane seeds. Two horns were also present along with bowls, a whetstone, weaving whorls and shears. Unusually, this Danish woman also had a wand or staff.

The Swedish scholar Dag Strömbäck has researched the possible identities of Scandinavian female burials that contain the same motifs as those of the British cunning-women. Strömbäck has interpreted the 'doctor's bag' and assorted items as being associated with a class of ancient women known in Scandinavia as Vanir. The etymology of the word Vanir remains unknown although it is sometimes seen speculated as referring to the proto-Indo European word for pleasure, although this is far from certain. From surviving descriptions of the Vanir, however, similarities with Mildþryþ and her British cousins can be discerned.

The Vanir were gifted with abilities of healing, magic, divination and prophecy and the word *seiðr* is used in Scandinavian research to describe this interrelated practice of healing and magic. The archeologist Neil Price describes their work:

'There were seiðr rituals for divination and clairvoyance; for seeking out the hidden, both in the secrets of the mind and in physical locations; for healing the sick; for bringing good luck; for controlling the weather; for calling game animals and fish.'

Further descriptions such as those recorded by Sturluson add to the identities and careers of the Vanir. From 'the girl' previously seen treating the warrior's potentially perforated stomach to the lively and detailed account of another woman, Thorbjiorg, in the saga entitled *Erik the Red*, Sturluson has fortunately retained a wealth of early Scandic stories that weave together a detailed picture of an organised hierarchy of women involved on national and community levels in medical, priestly and judicial roles.

He presents a vivid picture of the Vanir (also *Völva* in Old Norse) named Thorbjiorg who is called to an isolated community during a particularly harsh winter. Her job is clear; the village elders have invited her in her capacity as a Vanir with *seiðr* abilities to use rituals that will reveal the future fortune or ill of the community. When her work is concluded she will then continue her travels across the frozen North bringing similar help and counsel to other villages.

Sturluson states that Thorbjiorg (*Þorbjörg Lítilvölva*) is received as a priestess and treated with the upmost respect and hospitality. Despite the hostile time of famine, the villagers treat her to a lavish feast. She enters the humble hall dressed in finery including a sumptuous robe and cat-skin gloves all finished off with a lambskin bag hanging from her waist within which are her ritual healing items.

Following the feast, talk turns to the nature of the ritual that is to happen the following day and Thorbjiorg asks the villagers if they could send to her their cunning-woman to help with the ceremony and any necessary preparations. She is informed that unfortunately, they no longer have a cunning-woman although a girl called Gudrid was once so. Gudrid is summoned and explains to Thorbjiorg that she was indeed taught the seiðr arts by her step-mother, but having converted to Christianity she no longer practiced.

The story of Thorbjiorg and Gudrid exposes the potential hierarchical structure of Vanir and cunning-women in Britain and Scandinavia. At the top are those such as Thorbjiorg – although a healer, she is also a priestess particularly gifted in prophesying. She travels between villages and towns bringing supernatural intercedence in the form of ritual healings and knowledge of future events. Yet when she arrives in town she expects to find other women similarly gifted but on a local level. This second tier of cunning-women refers to those such as Gudrid and Mildþryþ.

Archaeology supports Sturluson's description of powerful Vanir travelling the lands, yet where his research focused upon Norway and Iceland, a grave discovered in Egtved in Denmark suggests this tradition reached further afield.

The body of a girl of just 16-18 years old was discovered in Egtved dating back 3400 years. From the tree rings of her wooden coffin, scientists can even state that she was buried in 1370 BC. Forensic analysis further reveals that she made long trips during her lifetime. Originally from Southern Germany she seems to have travelled around Northern Europe ending up in Egtved. Her jewellery, which was engraved with spiral symbols, has caused archeologists to speculate that she was a priestess of the ancient Scandinavian goddess cult of *Härn*. If so, then she may have been a Vanir similar to Thorbjiorg, travelling the land bringing healing, help and divine mediation.

Mildþryþ may therefore have been part of a once sophisticated hierarchical structure of medicine and religion. The priestly cast of Vanir acted as representatives of the goddess, traveling the communities bringing gifts of healing and prophesies to those in need. These women were well compensated for their work as the rich grave goods and literary descriptions portray. On a local level there existed women such as Gudrid and Mildþryþ, not so exulted but who nonetheless served their communities in a similar way and also received a certain amount of wealth in return. Often these women were the only ones buried with robes and grave goods within otherwise poor graveyards. It seems likely that these are the women Meaney and Dickinson have found in British graves and were interviewed for their remedies by the compilers of *Lacnunga* and *Bald's leechbook III*.

In the nineteenth century, the French historian and folklorist Léon Pineau sought to collect the old Danish ballads that were traditionally passed down orally through the generations. From the many songs he found, there is one entitled *Song of the Vanir*, which offers a deeper, stranger insight into their spiritual practices:

'She went to her chest, she dressed in silver.
She put gold on gold, she covered her two hands with it.
And all along the path, she taught him the runes upon her white
hand.
She taught him to change the weather, and to send the right
wind.'

In the song we are told how the Vanir adorns herself with the finest garments of silver and gold. Yet she is not preparing herself to prophesy for a community, attend a feast or heal the sick. Instead, she is leading a man along a 'path' where she instructs him in the secrets of the runes and teaches him further magical abilities such as how to command the weather. Myth is clear regarding the identity of this man, as there is but one who was taught the runes through the manner of an initiation – Woden.

It is told in the *Hávamál* that Woden received the secret of the runes whilst hanging upon the world tree *Ygdrassil,* where he descended into the otherworld on a path of initiation. When he emerged from his initiatory ordeal, he was also gifted with magical powers such as his ability to command the weather where 'With words alone he could quench fire, still the ocean in tempest, and turn the wind to any quarter he pleased'. Within the *Hávamál,* Woden describes his initiation and his grasping of the runes:

'I know that I hung
On the wind-blasted tree
All of nights nine,
Pierced by my spear
And given to Odin,
Myself sacrificed to myself
On that pole
Of which none know
Where its roots run.
No aid I received,
Not even a sip from the horn.
Peering down,
I took up the runes
Screaming I grasped them
Then I fell back from there.'

The parallel with Jesus's ordeal upon the cross is evident here and has often been remarked upon in popular reviews and academia alike. Recounted during a time when Norse paganism coexisted with Christianity, it is unsurprising that the two myths have blended, and so we hear Woden singing in his Rune Song - 'I know that I hung on a windy tree ... wounded with a spear.' Woden becomes the self-sacrificing god, his side pierced with a spear during his initiatory ordeal on nature's cross.

The similarity between Woden's pagan and Jesus's Christian experience, however, is contested and unresolved. Christian theologians can offer ample evidence to demonstrate it was Norse myth that first assimilated Christian facts. Yet the same is often argued the other way around. Donald Mackenzie for example, has traced pagan myth into darkest antiquity and explains:

'Only a Northern people living in close proximity to Arctic ice fields could have conceived of a chaos-gulf bounded on the North by a cold and darksome Nifelheim, and on the South by a warm and bright Muspelheim. Life begins to be when and where the ice-blocks are thawed'.

An exploration of post-ice-age mythology is beyond the scope of the current work, yet seeds of an earlier narrative than Woden's popular tapestry of tales of spiritual metamorphosis do exist. For example, we know from the *Sagas* that his initiation and journey into the otherworld were partly facilitated by a psychotropic substance known as flying potion. The recipe appears lost but henbane seeds, such as those discovered within the 'doctor's bag' of the Fyrkat cunning-woman, would have sufficed to induce the type of hallucinatory, shamanic experience required for such an initiation.

Woden's personal description of his initiatory experience, as recorded in the Sagas, is strident and confident, as we might expect from such a prominent god. He is quite clear that he received no help during his ordeal where he 'grasped' the runes 'whilst screaming'. Yet this is an exterior, observer's view of the event where Woden is relaying the details a prideful god would have his followers know. The *Song of the Vanir* hints at an earlier, rather different initiatory experience, one that a strident, prideful God may well wish to hide.

The *Song of the Vanir* indicates firstly, that Woden did receive help on his path to the runes, and that help was from a priestess. Further feminine themes emerge from the Sagas – in the *Poetic Edda* for example, Woden describes his experience of initiation as having felt as if he had been 'fertilised'. This use of overtly receptive, feminine language then continues, revealing an altogether different theory regarding the version of events that exist opaquely within the sagas.

In *Lokasenna* (Loki's quarrel) from Snorri's *Prose Edda*, Woden and Loki have a heated exchange and insults fly with abandon. For the culture of the time, the worst insult for a man was *argr* or *args* which in Old Norse means a man who engages in sexual activity similarly to a woman. Loki derides Woden stating that his initiation into the world of the Vanir where he gained the *seiðr* gifts of magic, '*oc hvgða ec þat args aþal*' (that to me is sodomy.) The reason for this insult is explained in the *Ynglinga* that says of the *seiðr* arts:

'it was not thought respectable for men to practise it; and therefore the priestesses were brought up in this art.'

The implication is that the knowledge Woden gained through his initiation was traditionally female knowledge alone, and for a man to practice it was to step outside of accepted societal norms. Woden therefore achieved a type of theological subterfuge; he claimed the highest godly throne by, in a sense, feigning himself as a woman. Loki even states that Woden had to adorn himself as a woman, in a '*seiðr*'s guise' to journey through his initiation and be reborn a god.

Although it has been counter-argued that references to Woden's transgender status come from the twelfth century historian Saxo Grammaticus who was born in Sjælland, Denmark, it does not follow that Saxo was doing any less than drawing upon the same oral heritage as Sturluson.

Archaeological evidence from Britain may also be supportive of this mixed gender theory. In Portway, Hampshire, which lies within Mildþryþ's tribal area, there was found the skeleton of a man adorned in female apparel and jewellery. Also dating from the sixth century, Henrietta Leyser explains that this is one of a small number of graves that could be described as 'third sex'. Wheat grains had been burnt and placed with the man, a custom eventually vetoed in the Penitential of Silos which states that this was a custom women did to men. Tellingly, in the same Penitential, it states of such men that, 'in the dance [they] wear women's clothes and strangely devise them'.

A Vanir teaching the craft of *seiðr* to Woden can thus be seen as a metaphor for a spiritual and cultural cosmological shift that occurred in Northern Europe between the fifth to twelfth centuries. This shift involved a movement from a predominantly female deity to a male deity with a consequential change of gender in the priestly caste.

In the Danish *Song of a Vanir* we therefore find preserved a vignette where a priestess of the old goddess is passing the sacred knowledge of *seiðr* craft (the knowledge and gifts of the divine), on to a man who, by way of the process, is consequently re-birthed as the god named Woden. Within the *Ynglinga* Saga we are even told that Freyja is most likely the Vanir who initiates Woden:

'Dóttir Njarðar var Freyja. Hún var blótgyðja. Hún kenndi fyrst með Ásum seið sem Vönum var títt.'

'The daughter of Njörðr. She was the priestess at the sacrifices. It was she who first taught the seiðr magic such as was practiced among the Vanir.'

The mythologist Joseph Campbell has found evidence for an initiatory tradition throughout Europe, the East and parts of Asia that saw the goddess who, as a teacher and guide, initiated men into adulthood. It might therefore be that the stories of Woden's initiation and morphic gender are linked to earlier rituals concerning maturing masculinity that became lost and devalued as Europe moved into the industrious Iron Age.

In surviving tribal societies, boys pass through an initiation to become men. Doing so provides the boy with a sense of role, purpose and security to become a useful and stable member of the tribe. The journey for girls into womanhood is different as their own bodies push them more overtly into the adult world and dictate, so it seems, their role as nurturer and life bringer. The female experience is visceral and overtly connected to the natural world, in sync with the lunar phase. This connection, standing outside of personal will, may have been viewed as magical, sacred and goddess-given.

If Campbell is correct, then we might expect to see women in the East and Asia fulfilling roles similar to the Vanir and cunning-women, especially when it comes to healing. Yet when we look to antiquity, it seems men such as Hippocrates and Galen dominate the medical world. A hieroglyphic carving discovered in a tomb near the Saqqara pyramid in Memphis, however, hints at a possible female heritage to the teachings of these great Greek physicians.

The inscription reads that a woman named Merit-Ptah was the 'Chief Physician', and dating to approximately 2700 BC, this makes her one of the first physicians ever recorded. To be labelled 'Chief' indicates hierarchy and structure and it is known that a medical school existed at the Temple of Neith in Sais that was run by women for the training of women only. Although the date of its inauguration is unknown, it was certainly in existence by the time another woman named Peseshet, was known to be teaching there three hundred years after Merit-Ptah. Peseschet was known as the 'Lady Overseer of the Lady Physicians' and is referred to in inscriptions as the 'King's Associate,' which suggests she was also personal physician of the monarch.

Although Egyptologist Barbara Watterson has argued that Merit-Ptah and Peseschet are exceptions, this misses an important fact: the early male figures of Egyptian medicine such as Imhotep practiced later than Merit-Ptah. Indeed, Egyptologist James Peter Allen contends that a woman pre-dating even Merit-Ptah whose name is unknown, ran the Sais school from at least 3000 BC. Allen further states that the Greeks equated Imhotep 'with their own god of medicine, Asklepios, although ironically there is no evidence that Imhotep himself was a physician'. It is possible that references to Imhotep as being a physician were appropriated from or confused with Merit-Ptah, whose inscription was curiously discovered near Imhotep's own tomb.

Egyptian female physicians therefore attended the king and taught medicine in schools. Further women studied and practiced such as Hatshepsut (1479-1458 BC), and a number of women named Cleopatra whose identities have become confused with each other. One stands out, however, and living during the Ptolemaic Period is known to have been a great influence upon the schools of Alexandria. From the second century BC, Greek physicians regularly reference her and cite her works. Galen (126-216) for example, is known to have consulted one Cleopatra.

Women in Egypt continued to practice as physicians into the fourth century until the rise of Christianity. Perhaps the most well-known was Hypatia of Alexandria (c. 370-415), who taught medicine, mathematics and astronomy. Her death at the hands of a Christian mob is often stated as marking the end of Classical Antiquity with Stephen Greenblatt arguing further that Alexandria's intellectual age died with Hypatia.

Recent research conducted by Susan Rasmussen has provided a possible remnant of this ancient female heritage of medicine surviving into the present era. Rasmussen spent time with the Tuareg people of the Sahara dessert. The Tuareg tribe is seminomadic and Rasmussen discovered that this Islamic tribe retains a pre-Islamic tradition of matrilineal descent along with a particular tradition of exclusively female physicians. These physicians are present today and she explains how 'in order to avoid challenging male Islamic authorities, women healers must keep a low profile and accept a specialized niche'. She explains that the tribe is contested today, with women becoming increasingly marginalised with regard to issues of ownership, descent and fertility. It is therefore likely that in some decades hence, the female physicians of the Tuareg will also disappear.

Chapter 7

The Cult of the Goddess

The mythologist Joseph Campbell has made an extensive study of humanity's changing relationship with deity and has discovered evidence from Paleolithic European cave art through to Neolithic tales, that common motifs of an ancient revered goddess are present.

In her book *Woman as Healer,* Jeanne Achterburg further explains how early goddesses such as the Egyptian Isis, Gula in Assyria, the Greek Demeter and Astarte, Nerthus from Germania, Freyja, Harn, and many others are simply superimpositions 'of a stronger personality on a long-existing deity' – for example, by tracing motifs from British mythology, Michael Enright has discovered that the Scandic Freyja is related to the British goddess Frig, and both may be emergent identities of an older Celtic goddess associated with weaving.

Campbell views goddess worship as a logical, intuitive response to our observed human situation – women were seen as the only 'giver of life' at a time when the biological contribution by the male was not completely understood. To our ancestors, this put women on an equal standing with nature itself, which provided everything required for life to flourish and exist. Campbell goes on to theorise four stages of creation myth. Once, there was a supreme goddess, reigning alone. She then gave birth to a male god. This male ruled beside her for a time before finally corrupting and subduing his mother and re-writing the creation stories as his own.

The name of this 'supreme' first goddess is lost, although in Europe and particularly Britain, there is evidence that one of her very early incarnations may have been as the goddess Eostre/Ēastre. The first mention we have of Eostre comes to us from the Venerable Saint Bede who wrote in his *An Ecclesiatical History of The English People* of 731 AD:

> 'In olden times the English people ... calculated their months according to the course of the Moon. April, Eosturmonath ... has a name which is now translated "Paschal month" and which

54

was once called after a goddess of theirs named Eostre, in whose honour feasts were celebrated in that month. Now they designate that Paschal season by her name, calling the joys of the new rite by the time-honoured name of the old observance.'

Bede lived most of his life in the North East of England and his treatise on English history is generally considered to be authoritative. The historian Patrick Wormald states that Bede is 'the first and greatest of England's historians'. Few find fault with Bede's authenticity, although some academics such as Charlotte Behr consider that Bede occasionally entwined myth with facts producing an interpretative rather than factual account.

As Easter stands as the most significant marker of Christian faith expressed within the story of Christ – his resurrection from the dead – it is understandable that many would support Behr's theory and side-line Bede's version of history. After all, Bede stood alone in his identification of Eostre as a British pagan goddess. This isolation has welcomed dissent, as it seemed uncomfortable to posit a pagan origin for Easter based upon the writings of just one man, and without archaeological or anthropological evidence of Eostre's existence, some even believe that Bede simply made her up.

Today, each Easter delivers newspaper articles concerning the controversy. Sometimes reporters call upon the validity of the Easter Bunny as an emblem of ancient pre-Christian origins. Increasingly, others are pulling in the opposite direction; in 2011, the *Guardian's* Adrian Bott compared Bede's mention of Eostre with the authenticity of Catweazle.

The acclaimed nineteenth century historian, mythologist and linguist Jacob Grimm, however, supports Bede's statement for the existence of the goddess Eostre. Grimm's extensive history of Germania was published in 1882 and entitled *Teutonic Mythology*. A notable linguist, he researched the etymology of *Ostern*, the German word for Easter and found it derived from the Old High German *Ostar*, both of which informed the Anglicised *Eostre*. *Ostar* became *Ostern* and *Eostre* similarly became Easter. Both terms, according to Grimm, refer to an ancient fertility goddess of Germanic origins:

'We Germans to this day call April *ostermonat*, and ... The great Christian festival, which usually falls in April or the end of March, bears in the oldest of [Old High German] remains the name *ôstarâ*. This *Ostrâ*, like the [Anglo Saxon] *Eâstre*, must in the heathen religion have denoted a higher being, whose worship was so firmly rooted, that the christian teachers tolerated the name, and applied it to one of their own grandest anniversaries.'

Grimm's linguistic research concerning the word *ôstarâ* begins to unpick an early identity for Eostre beyond Bede's account and so provides the evidence that has been missing. When we look at the word Eostre, we can quickly see the identity of a once great goddess emerging. In ancient Greek for example, the word *oîstros* meant something akin to passion and warmth and in later Italian, Portuguese and Catalan its derivative *estro* (and in French *œstre*) refers to the female reproductive cycle. In English oestrus is used, a word which also identifies the primary female sex hormone oestrogen.

These terms referring to passion and female fertility are cognate with the Proto-Indo-European root *hews,* meaning 'to shine'. The English word 'east', the direction of the rising sun also comes from this root and bears obvious similarity to 'Easter'. In German 'east' is *ost,* and is also therefore, similar to the German word for Easter, *Ostern.* There are countless examples of a rich linguistic heritage that links the word Easter to an ancient concept of light and fertility.

There is another tiny word that slips in with Easter and reveals further truth regarding this festival's pagan origins – Lent. In John MacArthur's *New Testament Commentary*, he states, 'The celebration of Lent has no basis in Scripture, but rather developed from the pagan celebration'. The monk Cassianus also remarked that the forty day's observance 'had no existence' in Scripture either. In English, the word lent comes from the Old Saxon *lentin* meaning the 'length of spring' from the Proto-Germanic *langatīnaz.* A strong theme is thus emerging that Richard Rives puts succinctly in his *Too Long in the Sun:*

> 'History records that spring festivals in honor of the pagan fertility goddesses and the events associated with them were celebrated at the same time as 'Easter'. In the year 399 A.D. the Theodosian Code attempted to remove the pagan connotation from those events and banned their observance ... Easter is not another name for the Feast of Passover and is not celebrated at the Biblically prescribed time for Passover. This pagan festival was supposedly 'Christianized' several hundred years after Christ.'

Grimm always maintained that Bede, a father of the church who kept 'heathenism at a distance', was an unlikely character to invent a pagan goddess as the origin of Easter. Perhaps Bede came into contact with groups still worshipping Eostre in her ancient aspect, or alternatively, he might have simply engaged in vigorous research and stated what to him seemed obvious.

The controversy may never end. Each religion will continue to claim this age-old spring festival as its own and one may wonder if it really matters and whether such arguments do anything but cloud the waters unnecessarily. Yet walk into almost any English church at Easter time and you will find traditions that do not occur in the Bible, Scripture or Judaism. Symbols of fertility such as eggs, both real and made of chocolate together with rabbits, hares and Easter bonnets all point to memories surviving in Britain from something other than the story of Christ's resurrection – vicars proudly give away chocolate eggs to children whilst planning in advance who will dance the Maypole on May Day. A pretty girl will soon be chosen to represent the goddess as May Queen, and along with her three attendants, will be paraded through the streets of small villages.

Eostre exists therefore, not as an identity to be found in sagas, songs and carvings, but in the expression of nature, which has survived in the words we use today to describe themes of fertility and life. The dance of life, death and rebirth plays out in countless creation myths from around the globe and finds its way into contemporary religious thought. It is an enduring human preoccupation. As the philosopher Alan Watts describes:

> 'The story of Easter is not simply a Christian story. Not only is the very name "Easter" the name of an ancient and non-Christian deity; the season itself has also, from time immemorial, been the occasion of rites and observances having to do with the mystery of death and resurrection among peoples differing widely in race and religion.'

An early goddess who can be found named in ancient sources is Nerthus, and it is by investigating the traditions surrounding her that we might re-construct a past when Eostre ruled alone. Nerthus appears fleetingly in the Nordic Sagas, predating the more famous Freyja and was a renowned healer. Carvings of her exist in Germany and Scandinavia dating into Palaeolithic times where she is often depicted with spirals and Celtic torque necklaces.

Like Eostre, she was a fertility goddess and the songs and tales tell us how she would appear in human form in order to mate with a human male. The selected man would be treated to a sacramental meal consisting of many different types of seed. These seeds were then cast back to the earth along with a blood sacrifice by way of the man's death. This is not just a story – in the Danish bogs there was discovered a man dating from 294 BC. Known as Tollund Man, his stomach contents revealed a final meal consisting of sixty-five different types of seed. Also, in the Irish county of Meath another man named the Moydrum Man dating from 2000 BC was discovered with his stomach full of sloe berry seeds. His body showed signs of ritual sacrifice and archaeologists, adding this find to others, suggest that this is evidence of an ancient tradition of regicide, whereby the king of the land is sacrificed to a triune fertility goddess following a symbolic marriage.

This archaeological evidence correlates with cultural narratives discovered by Joseph Campbell, narratives that span the whole ancient agrarian world and tell of kings being sacrificed to the goddess and then rising again for the next seasonal cycle.

Professor Adolf Jensen supports Campbell, explaining that these rites of kingly death and rebirth were inspired by observations of the natural world with its life and death cycles. The archaeologist Vere Gordon Childe clarifies further how these observations began in relation to natural cycles and became augmented and changeable when humanity moved from a wandering foraging culture to an agricultural one. He states that this change was 'the greatest in human history after the mastery of fire', and so it is reasonable to expect that this explosive revolution altered religious and cosmological narratives in extraordinary ways.

For the new agrarian societies, seeds and crops were of particular importance. Rituals surrounding their cultivation and harvest took on great significance for people now almost wholly dependent upon them. Cycles of birth, growth, harvest, death and rebirth became embedded at the heart of the community as people developed an intimate relationship with this process upon which their lives depended. Migration was no longer an easy option if crops failed, as the burgeoning towns developed infrastructure and boundaries in this new, domesticated world. Large groups of people living together enabled the evolution of new social structures – unity was important to prevent tensions, and religion with its supernatural adherences may have taken on a particularly organised, systemised flavour.

It is generally accepted by scholars such as Klaus Schmidt that the Turkish site of Gobekli Tepi marks the rise of agriculture and the death of our nomadic hunter-gatherer lifestyle. Sustained by agricultural domestic processes, Gobekli Tepi predates Stonehenge by 6000 years. At this time, the people of Gobekli Tepi were seeking a level of mastery over the natural world that was to that point unprecedented. Such radical change altered the myths. Stories required re-writing as people needed to begin understanding themselves and their environment in different ways.

THE CULT OF THE GODDESS

As this new way of life reached the northern lands Nerthus became responsible for securing a fertile soil with good crops to sustain the people throughout the season and following winter. When the blood sacrifice had been achieved, she was then carried through the land on a wagon that had been cleansed in the waters of a lake. These wagons were later laid to rest in the waters as a further gift to Nerthus, and her priestesses were buried in wagons too. The Roman historian Tacitus relays the belief of the Germanic 'barbarian' tribes regarding Nerthus and her wagon:

> 'On an island in the ocean is a sacred grove where a wagon stands, used for transporting the image of the goddess through the surroundings at *pax et quies* times when all fights rested and general peace reigned.'

A number of well-preserved wagon burials have been unearthed across Scandinavia. All are female and all are women of high wealth and status. A particularly fine example of such an inhumation was found at Oseberg, Norway and as Evy Johanne Håland suggests, 'points towards an association between the women in the grave and the fertility deity of the Viking Age.'

The re-writing or re-interpretation of a culture's creation myth and the gendered roles of its characters or archetypes is a powerful action. Joseph Campbell has identified this re-writing, specifically the subordination of the once great goddess, as a significant aspect of changing cultural frameworks. Creation myths are fundamental to humanity's quest to discover itself in relation to the universe, as they enable us to fathom our inner experiences and interpret them in relation to the wider world. Psychologically, myth enables humanity to place itself within a larger context of meaningful relationships, especially those with a deity.

Following years of research, Campbell believes that these creation stories reveal a 'unity of the race of man, not only in its biology but also in its spiritual history, which has everywhere unfolded in the manner of a single symphony'. Make significant alterations to a culture's notion of its genesis and eschatological outcome therefore, and you influence that culture in myriad ways.

Campbell has found similar motifs of a goddess being subdued by a male god within all cultural myths, existing within what Carl Jung might have called the 'collective unconscious' of humanity. Although aspects are culturally specific, the over-arching tales are deeply embedded and similar throughout the world. The psychoanalyst Marie Louise von Franz, a student of Jung, argues that the ancient myths survive today within our fairytales.

Another ancient goddess who is similar to those already listed such as Nerthus, Isis and Freyja came from Sumeria and was named Ianna. In Hebrew she was known as Asherah and Achterberg explains how the ancient Sumerian culture, the first culture we might describe as 'civilised' in today's terms, was the first to experience Campbell's notion of the diminution of their goddess:

> 'Until about 2000B.C., women participated fully in sacred activities, owned property and business, and, if they were unmarried, could serve as priestess-physicians. In examining the turning point of this relatively advanced civilization, we witness the transformation of the Sumerian feminine myth, the loss of women's connection to the divinity, and hence loss of recognition of their natural gifts in the realm of healing.'

Asherah, whose name means 'sacred tree', ruled with the Old Testament god Yahweh before he went completely solo. We know this because traces of Asherah and her earlier regal status still exist and have been found by archeologists. An inscription discovered in 1975 in the ancient Sinai site of Kuntillet Ajrud is written in Old Hebrew and invokes the protection of Yahweh and Asherah stating, 'I bless you by Yahweh, our guardian, and His Asherah.' The inclusion of the word 'His' is contested but appears to indicate a phase within belief when Asherah was queen consort to the strengthening Yahweh.

That she once ruled equally with Yahweh can be traced from Yahweh's connection with the older god El, who is overtly mentioned as Asherah's consort in the Syrian *Ras Shamra* texts. Biblical Scholar Mark Smith, a leading expert on the Dead Sea Scrolls and Near Eastern religion found that the texts reveal themes that 'belong to a shared or overlapping cultural matrix with the Hebrew Bible'. Although he concedes that 'the mists of time, camouflage a complex relationship between El and Yahweh', he is in general agreement with scholars that El was the original name for Yahweh, having given his name to the tribe of Isra*EL* and potentially, also to Allah.

According to research conducted by Frank Cross of Harvard, Asherah's original titles were 'Creatress of all the Gods' and 'Mistress of Sexual Rejoicing'. Cross believes that she originally functioned as a creatrix, a mother goddess. There are even surviving emblems of Asherah included in the Old Testament. As the 'Sacred Tree' she embodies the tree of life and knowledge so reminiscent of the Norse and Anglo-Saxon Norns who sit beneath the World Tree Ygdrasill, weaving the fates of humanity in Trinitarian form. Although the Old Testament prohibits the continued worship of Asherah stating, 'You shall not set up an asherah of any wood next to the altar of Yahweh your god' (Deut. 16:21), other scribes seem to have set out to include her surreptitiously:

> 'Her ways are pleasant ways and all her paths are peace. She is a tree of life to those who take hold of her, and happy are all who hold her fast.'
>
> (Proverbs 3:17.)

The archaeologist William Dever believes that Asherah was once worshipped in her own right by the ancient tribe of Israel as an early Cannanite fertility goddess but that this was, and continues to be, played down and her presence in Biblical scripture veiled.

When Asherah accepted a male consort and ruled together with the god Yahweh, they embodied complementary aspects of the natural and supernatural worlds. Asherah was healer, nurturer and life giver. Yahweh was a god of thunder and warrior might. When Asherah became demoted, something Professor Judith Hadley believes was occurring during the Old Testament era, and almost written out of the mythic structure of the Hebrew texts, Yahweh, now ruling alone, devoid of the balancing attributes of his Queen of Heaven became the vengeful warring god.

The ancient symbols of life and wisdom then altered accordingly. The tree of life, a symbol for Asherah found by archaeologists carved with her image in ancient sites became denied to humanity. Knowledge, once seen as a positive part of life became a serpent's curse where previously 'There was no trickery, wrath or deception. Knowledge was seen as a gift not a curse' (Achterberg).

The turning of the ancient creation myth from feminine to male had consequences that would ripple throughout the world. Oddly, however, Asherah might have made it to Hwicce country. In 1951 an ancient relief of a goddess was presented to Winchester College. The goddess was depicted standing upon a lion, naked and with the sun and crescent moon above her head. In her hands, she holds lotus blossoms and serpents. The scene is similar to many representations of Asherah yet unfortunately, 'No precise information is available concerning either its original acquisition or the date it reached England.' The college no longer has the artefact.

The demise of Asherah may be the first discernible point of gender conflict that gained momentum over thousands of years to eventually culminate in the European Witch Craze. Evidence from the Old Testament supports this progression as we find in Jeremiah a scene where local women and 'children gather wood, and the fathers kindle the fire, and the women knead dough to make cakes all for Asherah, the queen of heaven'. The women are interrogated regarding this practice and respond that 'since we stopped burning sacrifices to the queen of heaven and pouring out drink offerings to her, we have lacked everything and have met our end by the sword and by famine'.

As the questioning continues, Jeremiah focuses increasingly on the ungodly behaviour of women as being distinct from that of men. They are asked for example, whether they continue their traditions with their husband's approval, to which they respond in some disbelief:

'When we made offerings to the queen of heaven and poured out drink offerings to her, was it without our husbands' approval that we made cakes for her bearing her image and poured out drink offerings to her?'

The style of questioning and the specific focus on women as the instigators of ungodliness recalls the content and structure of the later Canon *Episcopi* and *Malleus Maleficarum,* both of which underpin and seek to legitimise, the witch trials. Both documents concern the problem of continuing pagan traditions of healing, magic and divination perpetuated by women under the auspices of a powerful goddess.

Chapter 8

Daughters of Eve

'all witchcraft comes from carnal lust, which is in women insatiable.'

Kramer, *Malleus Maleficarum*

A pagan who converted to Christianity in the fourth century made the first powerful step towards demonising Mildþryþ and recasting her tribal name as 'witch'. Born in 354 to parents Patricius and Monica, Aurelius would go on to become one of the greatest theologians and fathers of the Roman Church. By his death in 430 he was known as Augustine of Hippo, and to us he is simply Saint Augustine.

From his modest beginnings in the North African village of Thagaste, Augustine went on to study at the university in Carthage and it was whilst there that he encountered his most influential religious philosophy – Manichaeism. Its founder, the Persian prophet Mani, described Manichaeism as a 'religion of light'. Following a number of visionary revelations he experienced as a child, Mani developed his new religion with the aim of completing the teachings of the Buddha, Zoroaster and Jesus.

Manichaeism attracted the young Augustine who saw within its philosophy an elegant and intelligent interpretation of the cosmology of the sacred, which contrasted with what he had always viewed as a lack of intelligence in the tenets of Christianity. On his explorative path, inquiring into the deepest concerns of humanity Augustine had first been exposed to his father's paganism and his mother's Christian faith, both of which he rejected. Yet when he encountered the teachings of Mani, Augustine found a philosophy that appeared to answer what was for him a central and personal preoccupation – the issue of conflict between good and evil.

Mani had theorised two worlds in eternal conflict. There was the realm of light, which was spiritual, in contrast to the tormented physical reality of darkness. This view is generally called absolute dualism where two forces, both pre-eminent, are in a survival dance that never ends. Mankind is trapped between these battling forces and the battlefield is right here on Earth. The physical world therefore, is believed to be evil and in Christian terms, the devil is seen as equally powerful to God.

The construction of Mani's hierarchy of creation is elaborate, yet this complexity gave to the young Augustine the intellectual vigour he hungered for and which seemed to elevate his parent's paganism and Christianity to a higher level. Augustine was a Manichean for nine years until he heard the preaching of a Christian inspired by pagan dualism – Bishop Ambrose.

To call Ambrose a dualist is perhaps a little uncharitable, but his adoption of pagan Neo-Platonist philosophy mixed with Christian thought, was in many ways an odd hotchpotch of styles. The Neo-Platonists were followers of Plotinus, a pagan dualist who had brought together teachings from two of the greats; Plato and Aristotle. Plotinus's interpretation of dualism was not, however, as absolute as that of the prophet Mani. Where Mani viewed good and evil forces as equal and pre-eminent, Plotinus theorised a single unifying principle from which they both emerged. Neo-Platonists term this unifying principle 'The One' and when combined with the emerging forces of light and dark, a form of Trinitarianism is created.

Ambrose's Neo-Platonism, which seemed to bridge a gap between dualist Manichaeism and monotheistic/Trinitarian Christianity impressed Augustine. He converted to Catholicism and was baptised by Ambrose during the Easter Vigil of 24 April 387. Yet his early Manichean beliefs fuelled an unusually extreme interpretation of Christian Scripture, which was to have catastrophic consequences for the Hwicce, cunning-women, women generally, and for the way our modern Western minds experience our world and ourselves.

Augustine's re-interpretations of Scripture that follow his conversion are rooted deeply in his early life and experiences. It is clear from his writings that Augustine experienced a duality to his inner nature that peppered his entire theology. In his *Confessions* he explains:

> 'So these two wills within me, one old, one new, one the servant of the flesh, the other of the spirit, were in conflict and between them they tore my soul apart.'

Augustine was a man deeply aware of his own internal conflict. His own battle with what we might today call 'the shadow' or 'inner demons' emerged from his experience of what he terms his 'muddy concupiscence of the flesh', which motivated his behaviour as a young man when he fathered a child with a woman he later abandoned. He speaks of 'the remembrance whereof I am now ashamed' and he struggles to understand the motives for his behaviour:

> 'What then was this feeling? For of a truth it was too foul: and woe was me, who had it. But yet what was it? Who can understand his errors?'

By seeking to understand his own errors and aberrant behaviour, Augustine, following his conversion to Christianity, is confronted by the problem of evil; how can an all-loving, omnipotent god allow evil and suffering to exist? This problem and how to solve it sits beneath Augustine's entire philosophy and interpretation of Scripture, preoccupying his life. For example, he wondered how a good god could allow innocent babies to be born with distressing diseases and deformities. Augustine ultimately concludes that 'the only innocent feature in babies is the weakness of their frames; the minds of infants are far from innocent'. It then necessarily follows that if born sinful, then this sin is inherited, genetically through its mother and here lies Augustine's foundation for his doctrine of original sin that led him to finally write in his *De genesi ad litteram*:

> 'What is the difference whether it is in a wife or a mother, it is still Eve the temptress that we must beware of in any woman … I fail to see what use woman can be to man, if one excludes the function of bearing children.'

Stacy Magedanz writes in her guide to Augustine's *Confessions* that Augustine viewed women as obstructions to living a godly, righteous life. From his mother, who stood in his way of going to Rome, to the pagan Empress who stood against Augustine's mentor Bishop Ambrose, women were blocks on the path to salvation. As Magedanz explains:

> 'Augustine's obsession with sex is in one sense an obsession with women, and it is the last obstacle to his full embrace of Christianity. Women in the *Confessions* are only lovers or mothers.'

His *Confessions* make scant mention of his parents except to lament their lack of discipline, a neglectful error Augustine believes, that gave purchase to Satan within his soul, resulting in his immoral behaviour. For example, the only interest his father Patricius had was in his education, as Augustine explains:

'Who did not extol my father, for that beyond the ability of his means, he would furnish his son with all necessaries for a far journey for his studies' sake? For many far abler citizens did no such thing for their children. But yet this same father had no concern how I grew towards Thee, or how chaste I were; so that I were but copious in speech, however barren I were to Thy culture, O God'

Augustine then continues to describe that whilst on a year's break from his studies during which his father worked hard to provide more money for him to return to university, Patricius nonetheless failed his son by his reaction to his blossoming manhood:

'But while in that my sixteenth year I lived with my parents, leaving all school for a while (a season of idleness being interposed through the narrowness of my parents' fortunes), the briers of unclean desires grew rank over my head, and there was no hand to root them out. When that my father saw me at the baths, now growing towards manhood, and endued with a restless youthfulness, he, as already hence anticipating his descendants, gladly told it to my mother; rejoicing in that tumult of the senses wherein the world forgetteth Thee its Creator, and becometh enamoured of Thy creature, … Woe is me!'

The vignette here described is not so unfamiliar to us today. Having worked hard to provide an education for his son, Patricius notices with pride that Augustine is now becoming a man and will soon be able to marry and have a family of his own. Where one person might see a loving parent doing their best, Augustine looks back and sees a father enamoured with 'the very basest things'.

It seems to Augustine that Patricius is concerned only with the superficial aspects of this earthly life – education, opportunity, marriage, children, and sees no profits in life beyond these meagre rewards. Patricius, Augustine explains, has put his focus in 'the hope of learning, which both my parents were too desirous I should attain' rather than on serving God. Augustine continues, stating that parental discipline was consequently 'slackened to me, beyond all temper of due severity, to spend my time in sport, yea, even unto dissoluteness in whatsoever I affected.' This lack of discipline then led him to sin whereby 'I could not discern the clear brightness of love from the fog of lustfulness'.

Augustine's early family life stands as a thematic psychological influence beneath his later theology and re-interpretations of Scripture. Today he is referred to as the Father of Christian psychology as he managed to form a theological concept of the mind of God which in turn created, according to theologian Ellen Charry, a biblically inspired:

'understanding of the psyche, the self, the soul. In modern technical theological language this is referred to as theological anthropology, Christianity's reading of human nature. It offers an analysis of the soul's strengths and weaknesses, and suggests means for strengthening, repairing, and cultivating it.'

Before Augustine could provide a convincing theological anthropology, however, he needed to distance himself from Manichaeism. The Church considered the philosophy of Mani, which influenced later groups such as the Cathars and Bogomils, blasphemous and it is understandable that Augustine would wish to distance himself from his previous dualism as successfully as possible.

Where he had previously seen elegance in dualism, which balanced good and evil, he now saw a deeply rooted problem, as his new religion taught that God is all-good and unitary. Perhaps another would have let the issue rest but for a man peculiarly preoccupied with his own internal shadow, an all-good God awakened a conflict within Augustine which grasped his conscience and mind for the rest of his life. He would ask whether, if God was an all-good supreme deity, then how was it that evil could exist? It was a problem, and Augustine's reasoning would have some devastating effects on Mildþryþ's profession and on women generally – effects that reverberate into the present day.

Augustine grappled with deeply troubling ontological and cosmological quandaries as he sought to resolve evil within the auspices of an all-good and powerful god. Also, he wanted to know the facts – just how powerful was Satan, and where were his boundaries of activity? Augustine began to think retroactively as he formulated a hypothesis: as God was good and all-powerful, then it must necessarily follow that God permits evil to exist. If he permits it, then it must, in some way, be good. Consequently, Satan must be a positive instrument within God's wider, mysterious plan. So far so good, but the details would prove less straightforward.

Augustine now needed to propose a good purpose for evil if his theory was to become coherent. Also, he needed to prove that Satan, although powerful, was not some sort of equal to God as his previous dualistic faith had taught. Yet by striving to distance himself from Mani's teachings, it seems that he might have overly focused on the very dualism he wished to denigrate, and let Satan return through the back door, disguised in female clothes. This is because Augustine was about to make Eve the perpetrator of irreconcilable, endemic and infectious sin.

Augustine still had some way to go before he was ready to impose upon Eve the burden of sin. First of all, he needed to take the pressure off Satan and so he theorised that Satan must be the tool God uses to bring about the correction and conversion of humans so they might be brought back home to God. But this begged the question – why aren't humans already at home in paradise, enjoying the creation where everything was 'good' and carefree? Human beings, Augustine continued, were given a wonderful gift by God; free will. Yet this gift came with responsibility and certain dangers that human beings, due to a degree of capriciousness, were curious to explore. It is from this notion of capricious mutability that Augustine put forth his doctrine of original sin.

The foundation for his doctrine was that although free will is a good, benevolent virtue, it nonetheless gives the potential for moral corruption through disordered thinking. Nothing is of itself evil (it can't be in a world created by an all-good god), yet evil can manifest when we, God's creations, become confused. Philip Carey of the Christian Eastern University explains this with a useful metaphor – if a person betrays their best friend for thirty pieces of silver, there is nothing inherently evil about the money or event. The evil has emerged from the disordered mind that put the value of the money above the relationship with the friend. This is how evil works. As theologian Jesse Couenhoven explains – according to Augustine 'human beings are born misrelated to God'.

Augustine continued; so far he had found intelligent reasoned arguments for some of the most difficult questions that lay at the heart of Christian doctrine: the nature of evil, the role of Satan and the reason for sin. Yet Augustine then made a radical step when exploring the original sinners of humanity – Adam and Eve.

He explains Adam's sinfulness at eating the apple as being part of human capriciousness stating that Adam 'sinned because he willed to sin' but that, 'original sin is something else' and babies, born of their mothers, 'contract it' like a disease, 'without any will of their own'. Original sin is thus a biological infection inherited by each subsequent generation through its parent's sexual intercourse, enslaving every human being to guilt and shame due to 'the guilt from our origin which was contracted by birth'. This elevates sin to a whole new level which had never before been theorised.

This radical, biological sin builds upon the capriciousness of normal sin to explain what Augustine terms in his *The Perfection of Human Righteousness* as 'un-willed' sin. This does not result from the misrelationship and confused curiousness of Adam and Eve but from female 'carnal concupiscence' which results from a desire for the forbidden.

Although Augustine did not invent the notion of original sin (it can be seen to have evolved from pagan origins), theologian Gerald Bray states that no evidence of the doctrine of original sin as we would understand it today, exists before Augustine. He was the first to formulate it as dogma with a wholly negative interpretation that included overt shame, guilt and the evil status of women and sex.

Before Augustine, Judaic and early Christian interpretations of Genesis did not include these negative elements. Sex was viewed as sacred; after all 'God saw all that he had made, and it was very good' (Genesis 1:31). Yet Augustine targeted the act of sexual intercourse as the locus of continued sinful infection that corrupts us all and holds us away from the love of God. This had the consequence of meaning that Jesus could no longer have been conceived normally. He had to have been conceived without the passing on of infectious sin, so it had to have been an Immaculate Conception. Yet this led to a further consequence – Mary had to be sinless too, or else she could pass on the infection. So now, Mary also had to have been the product of Immaculate Conception. The psychologist Jeanne Acterberg describes this type of religious reasoning as involving 'gyrations of logic'.

The importance of the radical stance of Augustine in this regard cannot be underestimated. Previous theologians, including the first century St Paul, had a less negative view of sin. Paul's view is based on Jesus's saying that, 'Man shall not live on bread alone, but on every word that comes from the mouth of God' and that, 'sin shall no longer be your master, because you are not under the law, but under grace' (Romans 6:14). This means that sin is primarily a matter of spiritual virtue, not physical genetics. By making it physical, Augustine made sex, birth and women, unclean, despite Ezekiel 18:19-20, which states clearly that the child does not inherit its father's sin. For Augustine, however, sin is the mother's domain.

By the fifteenth century, the view that women were predisposed to carnality resulted in perhaps the most notorious question of Kramer's *Malleus Maleficarum* which includes the following:

> 'The reason determined by nature is that [a woman] is more given to fleshly lusts than a man, as is clear from her many acts of carnal filthiness. One notices this weakness in the way the first woman [Eve] was moulded, because she was formed from a curved rib, that is, from a chest-rib, which is bent and [curves] as it were in the opposite direction from a man; and from this weakness one concludes that, since she is an unfinished animal, she is always being deceptive.'

By conceiving the new understanding of original sin as genetic, Augustine was able to theorise a further unpleasant consequence, that of the 'fall' of man. This was a new concept at the time. Previously, although Adam and Eve had been denied continued paradise, they were not viewed as 'fallen' but rather 'separated' as in Ephesians 4:18 where 'They are darkened in their understanding and separated from the life of God'. This is not an irreconcilable condition but could be corrected by turning to God. For Augustine, however, this was a change in state, which corrupted our very ontology. Humanity literally fell into a non-spiritual form. This extreme separation recalls the dualism of Mani.

According to Augustine, the greatest villain in the 'fall of man' and 'original sin' is not Satan, but Eve. In Augustine's thesis, a very important point is that the serpent, the devil, is not inherently evil. Satan was a great angel of God who through his own disobedience fell from grace. Yet this was just disordered thinking. Satan was good and chose to love himself, which is also good, yet he was mistaken when he valued self-love above his love for God. Satan was a normal sinner.

Eve, similarly to Satan, through her own capriciousness disobeys God, putting her in the same category as Satan. Yet Eve goes one step further by tempting Adam into having sex and it is this act that inaugurates original sin, condemning us all to a fallen state. Eve, the first woman, was worse than Satan.

The picture was not always so dark. In the earlier Sumerian version of genesis, the serpent was a positive symbol bringing the gift of knowledge and wisdom rather than the deceiver, tempting Eve with knowledge from the tree. Where once her eating of the apple represented an initiation into wisdom, it became in the Hebrew reworking of the myth a symbol of corruption and disobedience to God. Therefore, although the Hebrew texts may have begun the process of diminishing women, it was not until Augustine that this became dogma, locked into a dangerous, destructive narrative of woman as devil and eventually, witch.

With the doctrine of original sin now firmly established and focused upon the aberrant behaviour and nature of woman, the path was then clear to formulate laws and further dogma to help people avoid this genetically inherited damnation. Eve's disobedience became a pivotal example of how not to behave and so any disobedience to the Church was now viewed as equally diabolical and worthy of penance or punishment. Unquestioning obedience was the only choice. The Church would become the disciplining parent Augustine had wished for himself.

Yet may one not counter that the Roman Church reveres Mary, positioning her within the divine family? Unfortunately, the character and status of Mary does little to repair the damage done to the nature of woman. As the nineteenth century historian Jules Michelet explains:

> 'By a monstrous perversion of ideas, the Middle Ages regarded the flesh in its representative, woman (accursed since Eve) as radically impure. The Virgin, exalted as virgin, and not as Our Lady, far from raising actual womanhood to a higher level, degraded it, starting men on a path of a barren, scholastic idea of purity that only led to ever greater and greater absurdities of verbal subtlety and false logic.'

Due to the doctrine of original sin, Mary, mother of Christ could not be allowed to be a real woman, she had to be something removed, isolated and fundamentally different from the actual, shameful, diabolically 'perilous object' – according to Saint Jerome – that is woman.

We cannot know for sure if Augustine set out to particularly condemn women. It may simply be that unconscious content from his feelings of shame regarding his past lustfulness, his unclaimed son and heretical beliefs bubbled up and coloured his sincere desire to explain the nature of evil. Yet the consequence this had for women was devastating and we can say that he seemed unperturbed by this. When speaking of sin and evil, Augustine often used feminine pronouns to put his point across:

> '[Lust] is the daughter of sin, as it were; and whenever it yields assent to the commission of shameful deeds, it becomes also the mother of many sins.'

Augustine's grappling with duality has continued to dwell in the depths of Church dogma well into the present day, creating an internal conflict that is not easily resolved. The very concept of a loving god inspires a powerful symbol of love, nurture, caring and forgiveness, which are qualities most often associated with the feminine archetype. Male gods and their archetypes have mostly emerged as warring, hunting and authoritarian. This is not to say that gender archetypes cannot evolve; they do and they should, but, at the depth of dogma, are they doing so effectively or are they stagnant, confused and causing neurosis?

This raises an important social issue. How we experience divinity through the dominant religion of the day informs how we view ourselves, and our place within the universe. By theorising an inherently fallen, evil and unclean state for humanity, perpetuated by female carnality, Augustine's logic resulted in an enduring core belief of loss and guilt at the heart of our physical life. Core beliefs are typically hidden under positive attributes that do little to mask the festering conflict beneath.

Chapter 9

The Problem of Truth

St Augustine of Canterbury (534-604 AD) carried on the work of his namesake and came to Hwicce country in the summer of 603 within the Gregorian mission to convert the Anglo-Saxon pagans and Celtic Christians to Roman Christianity. Bede reports that:

> 'Augustine, with the help of King Ethelbert, drew together to confer with him the Bishops and Doctors of the next provinces of the Britons at a place which is called to this day, Augustine's Ac (Oak), on the borders of the Hwiccas and the West Saxons.'

Roman Bishops met with British Bishops and 'doctors' at a great tree that became known as Augustine's Oak, which may have stood in the Saxon villages of either Holy Oak or Mitre Oak on the Hwicce borderland. The story unfolds that the British Bishops refused to adopt the new Romanised version of Christianity and instead sought the counsel of a local hermit who suggested a second meeting, advising the British that should Augustine stand to greet them, then they should accept his offer and terms, but should Augustine fail to stand in greeting, then they should reject. Augustine did not stand and so the Hwicce rejected him.

By the time Augustine of Canterbury was standing under that oak tree on the edge of Hwicce territory, Augustine of Hippo had already written and published his four books on Christian Doctrine in the fourth to fifth centuries. The work, which included his new interpretation of Genesis and original sin, was designed to encourage and tutor his fellow clergy in the correct interpretation, teaching and defending of the Scriptures. Yet this work did not emerge in isolation.

Saint Augustine was in political collaboration with Theodosius the Great (347-395) to formally unite Constantine's Nicene Christianity with the State of Rome. The Old Testament inclination towards a divinely sanctioned Kingship was politically attractive and provided templates of governmental power for law making and tax collection. This enabled a political structure under the auspices of a divinely associated council of clergy that was desirable for the Empire of Rome. As Will Durant explains in his 1994 book *Caesar and Christ:*

> 'When Christianity conquered Rome: the ecclesiastical structure of the pagan church, the title and the vestments of the pontifex maximus, the worship of the Great Mother goddess and a multitude of comforting divinities, the sense of super sensible presences everywhere, the joy or solemnity of old festivals, and the pageantry of immemorial ceremony, passed like maternal blood into the new religion, and captive Rome conquered her conqueror. The reins and skills of government were handed down by a dying empire to a virile papacy.'

To this end, Theodosius, also inspired by Ambrose, Bishop of Milan, issued the Edict of Thessalonica in 380, which declared that Nicene Christianity, as forwarded by Constantine, was to be the only legitimate Imperial religion. By 393, he had banned pagan practices from state events and dissolved the status of the Roman Vestal Virgins. Theodosius' agenda was the eradication of paganism and Augustine was to justify that eradication morally and theologically.

The second century Roman writer Suetonius labelled Christianity as a *malefica superstitio* (a malignant superstition) and Caecilius described it as a 'subversive sect that threatens the stability of the whole world.' Before Constantine, Christians were accused of secret rites and abnormal sexual activities – it was told that they worshiped the head of ass and revered the animal's genitalia whilst cannibalising human infants. Yet Augustine's intellectual vigour would soon turn these allegations onto the accusers themselves – a kind of tit for tat perhaps, except that in the hands of a religion that viewed women as inherently sinful, this re-labelling of earlier beliefs, especially those revering the sacredness of women, would prove particularly damaging.

Asherah was not welcome, and the pagans of Europe who wouldn't let go of their female orientated practices needed to be dealt with. Yet a problem was evident to Augustine: cunning-women healed people and eased their distress, and logically, this seemed very good.

Augustine needed to demonstrate that although the results achieved by cunning-women were beneficial, they were nonetheless evil due to the capricious nature of women, and so, their healing and help were not 'good' at all. He used two particular passages from the Bible to illustrate what he believed to be examples of the false religious or supernatural experience that cunning-women provided.

The first is the story concerning the raising of Samuel's spirit for King Saul, who reigned in the eleventh century BC as the first monarch of the Kingdom of Israel and Judah (although this is today contested by archaeological and anthropological evidence). It's a story commonly known today as the Witch of Endor.

So the biblical account goes, Saul, on the brink of battle with the Philistines was fearful and unsure of what to do. He appealed to God but received no reply and so he wished that Samuel were there to guide and advise him, yet Samuel had died some years previously in Ramah. So Saul asks of his servant, 'Seek me a woman that hath a familiar spirit, that I may go to her, and inquire of her' (1 Samuel 28:7).

Following some enquiries, Saul's servant reports back that there was a medium at Endor. Unfortunately for Saul, he had outlawed the practice of mediumship and if caught seeking counsel from one he might be labelled a hypocrite and cause damage to his reputation. So a plan was devised to sneak away to Endor in the dark of night and in disguise.

Saul arrives at the woman's home after dark and asks her to 'conjure up' a spirit for him. Yet the woman answers, 'you know what Saul has done, how he has cut off those who are mediums and spiritualists from the land. Why are you then laying a snare for my life to bring about my death?' Saul then gives her his assurance that 'As the Lord lives,' no harm will come to her.

Using adjurations, the medium conjures the spirit as Saul requests and she tells him that a 'divine spirit' is coming up from the floor, coalescing into the form of an old man. When Saul identifies this to be none other than Samuel the woman realises Saul's deceit, but Saul reassures her, 'do not be afraid'.

We can only imagine what Saul was hoping to hear from his ghostly advisor, but we can be sure it was not the prophesy of doom he then received. After reprimanding Saul for his failure to obey God and go to war with the Amalekites, Samuel goes on to deliver his famous prophecy; Saul and his sons will all die in battle the very next day.

We are given no description of the medium. Many modern popularisations paint her as we might expect – crone-like and grizzled with a long moth-eaten robe. The final scene from this small vignette does portray something of her character though, as in the face of Saul's distress at hearing such shocking fortune, the woman is immediately compassionate, and urges him to take some food. The distressed king resists but is gently encouraged by the medium to think of his strength and take time to recover and fortify himself. She also reminds him that although his request had put her in danger, she helped him nonetheless. We are told that he 'listens' and partakes of a good meal of bread and veal that she has prepared. Unfortunately, this was to be King Saul's final evening meal. The prophesy was correct and the following day, when Saul realised his sons had all been slain during the battle, he fell upon his own sword.

Augustine saw the difficulty inherent in this story. The problem being, that Saul had consulted a woman known to be a medium or prophetess, and her prophecy had been the truth. Augustine saw how people could therefore be mistaken in concluding that female 'magic' was beneficial and delivered truths. Even more, that it might be divinely inspired.

A second story further exemplified what he saw as a misunderstanding regarding the nature of woman's gift for prophecy. In Acts 16:16 we find the following tale:

> 'One day as we were going to the place of prayer, we were met by a slave girl with a spirit of clairvoyance, who earned a large income for her masters by fortune-telling. This girl followed Paul and the rest of us, shouting, "These men are servants of the Most High God, who are proclaiming to you the way of salvation."'

Again, Augustine was troubled that a statement of truth, in this case the correct identification of Paul and his companions, had been uttered by a woman known for clairvoyance and prophecies. He felt that these two stories in particular represented the problem with paganism and were the reason why so many people held on to their pagan beliefs and continued to consult cunning-women. If magic and prophecy, which formed a large part of pre-Christian cosmology and healing, were useful and truthful, why would people wish to alter their beliefs and practices from ones that worked well for them and obey instead the Nicene religion of Theodosius? This was his dilemma.

That people were seeking the counsel of gifted women like Mildþryþ from Old Testament times to the Anglo-Saxon period, gives some insight into Augustine's concern. He needed to demonstrate that such women were not powerful and if they seemed so, it was a false illusion inspired by the devil. Only Christ and his representatives held spiritual power within Church and State. Mildþryþ and her kind had to be dealt with.

He reasoned that the spiritual, supernatural encounters portrayed in the biblical stories might have revealed true answers, but this was simply a case of 'spiritual fornication' with demons. What appeared to be good and truthful was in fact dark and evil. Augustine was about to eloquently and persuasively turn the whole cosmology of Northern Europe upside-down.

Due perhaps to his previous adherence to the gnostic Mani, Augustine was at great pains to differentiate and distance Nicene Roman Christianity from everything else – early esotericism, Gnosticism, Paganism, Mithraism and other forms of Christianity were all heralded as heretical. Within his work on Christian Doctrine, Augustine's implicit methodology to achieve Theodosius' political aims was to focus upon the genesis of religious experience itself. He was interested in establishing a clear understanding regarding the aetiology of spiritual encounters in order to teach the common people to discern between correct and good religious experiences and deceptive ones inspired by the devil. This was the next pivotal step that would ensure Mildþryþ's demise.

This is not to say that concern regarding 'black magic' was new. On the contrary, using magic to cause harm was always shunned within the pagan world. Within Mildþryþ's healing books are many remedies used by cunning-women to thwart the attentions of evil doers and their curses. For example, in *Lacnunga* we find 'a good drink against every evil' (*godne drænc wið ælcum yfele*) that explains that no matter where the curse has taken root, be it in the head or wherever else, the physician should:

'genim þu saluian leaf ond rudan leaf ond heldan leaf ond finoles cerfillan leaf ond hegeclifan leaf ond persoces leaf ond reads seales leaf, ealra efenfela, cnoca hy tosomme ond lege on wine oððe on hluttran ealað, ond wring þonne anre tide ær þu þe wille blod lætan, beþa þe þonne þa hwile to hatum fyre ond læt yrnan þone drænc into ælcan lime, gif þu him ænige hwile befylgest, þu ongist þæt he is frymful to beganne.'

'take sage's leaves and rue's leaves and tansy's leaves and fennel's and chervil's leaves and cliver's leaves and peaches leaves and red willow's leaves, and the same amounts of all, pound them together and lay them in wine or clear ale, and strain the herbs off and take an amount of honey and sweeten the drink, drink it then at the time you wish to bleed yourself, bathe yourself the while then before a hot fire and let the liquid run onto each limb. If you do this for a length of time you will see its usefulness.'

In a world where disease was generally viewed as being caused by external supernatural factors, salves and rituals designed to protect against curses and remedy evil would have been a frequent part of Mildþryþ's job. Taking a defensive, pro-active stance against the threat of curses is evident from many remedies where 'holy salves' and amulets are being made to fight evil magic. A number of curses have been preserved from Old Norse and Old English, so we can be certain such actions were of very real concern to our ancestors. For them, magic could be black or white and cunning-women worked to remedy the darkness.

What Augustine managed to do, versed as he was in the power of dualism, was in this instance to collapse the distinction between 'black' and 'white' magical practices so that in time, any benevolent woman using herbs for healing was doing so from a basis of demonic collaboration. Thus, he delineated the origins of supernatural experience and spiritual aid. It was very simple – should you require any sort of medical help or spiritual guidance and go to a cunning-woman, then you are consorting with the devil and his maidens. If you approach a priest, you'll be fine, even if the former can heal you and the latter cannot. In his *Christian Doctrine* he explains:

> 'all the amulets and remedies … whether these consist of incantations, or certain marks … or the business of hanging certain things up and tying things to other things. The purpose of these practices is not to heal the body, but to establish certain secret or even overt meanings.'

Healing is no longer the purpose of the ancient rituals. Something else is happening instead. The ritualistic and protective elements of Mildþryþ's work are being identified here as having secret or even overt meanings that are not to do with healthcare. The implication becomes obvious as Augustine's text continues, stating that physicians using any type of intervention without calling upon Christ are in a pact with demons and even if one such as Mildþryþ cures a patient, it is not good, as the cure has been achieved by virtue of the devil. Therefore, when the Gregorian conversion journeyed to Mildþryþ's home in the sixth century, it was already established that protective amulets and the like were the tools of 'foolish old women'.

What Augustine achieved was to re-interpret the role of women within the narrative of worldly evil and then, attack the nature of their pre-Christian magical activities as black magic, which, as most traditions have affirmed, is evil. This was a carefully conceived and often overlooked piece of theological wrangling that inspired future, overtly hostile Canon Law against pagan women generally, be they actually practicing the dark arts or healing the sick with herbs and protective amulets.

The Christian Church was born into a world where Jewish and Greco-Roman religious practice supported and utilised magical ritual to bring order and agency to the human condition. It is through religious and spiritual beliefs that mankind has assuaged its fears by empowering feelings of agency in the face of disease and disasters. It is also how we manage to live within the shadow of mortality. Evil seems to surround us. Evil also appears to have power over us, striking randomly to inflict pain, suffering and death. How we respond to these threats and assuage our fears necessarily affects our feelings of autonomy within the world.

Psychological and emotional agency is an important aspect of human mental health and societal structure. Our very identities and social interactions emerge from these core beliefs. The psychologist Albert Bandura put forward a useful model of 'emergent interactive agency' to explain how a complex reciprocal process in relation to environmental and personal factors motivates human beings. This means that our personal feelings of control and freedom, so important for our coping strategies in a hostile world, are directly linked to external influences such as culture, society and one may add, mythic and cosmological structures of belief. Alter these foundational structures of influence and it is possible to manipulate the mental health of society by controlling their experience of personal agency.

Where the people had previously found hope and confidence within the services offered by Mildþryþ and her kind, Saint Jerome now commended Augustine for establishing 'anew the ancient faith' by specifically focusing upon differentiating Mildþryþ's practices as being false superstition in relation to the superior and true religion of Christianity. So Mildþryþ's herbal healing and the rituals surrounding it, such as the binding of plants to the body, are now overt sorcery:

'Se wisa agustinus cwæð þæt unpleolic sy þeah hwa læcewyrte ðicge; ac þæt he tælð to unalyfedlicere wigelunge. gif hwa þa wyrt on him becnytte buton he hi to þam dolge gelecge; ðeahhwæðere ne sceole we urne hiht on læcewyrtum besettan; ac on þam ælmihtigum scyppende þe ðam wyrtum þone cræft forgeaf.'

'The wise Augustine said that it is not dangerous if someone eats a medicinal herb, but he censures it as an unlawful sorcery if he binds the herb onto himself, unless he lays it on a wound; however,

we ought not to place our hope in medicinal herbs, but in the
Almighty Creator, who gave that power to the herbs.'
(Homily for the *Passio Sancti Bartholomei*, ed. Clemoes, p. 450.)

The result of Augustine's re-interpretation of Scripture in conformity with Theodosius' political agenda was to move the locus of personal agency into absolute obedience to the Church. Even if Mildþryþ was benevolent, helpful, wise and good, this was a deception of the devil as the new theological stance re-branded women as essentially evil and pre-disposed to cavorting with demons. Using the problem of evil as an overarching theme, the theology was now in place to describe Mildþryþ as an agent of Satan by virtue of her sex and her status as physician. As the later William of Malmesbury wrote in 1140 regarding the so called 'witch' of Berkeley, she acted, 'not by divine miracle, but by infernal craft,' and was furthermore, 'addicted to sorcery'. Augustine's stance was well and truly adopted.

A reworking of mythic identities was now underway. Darkest archetypes that had been part of pagan thought and Judaic supernatural cosmology became joined together. Previous categorisations that had discerned between good and bad supernatural practices and practitioners were now defunct. There was just one archetype that included both the benevolent cunning-women and the black magic sorcery so feared by all pre-Christian traditions. Good had become bad. Mildþryþ was longer a physician, she was a witch.

Above: The beautiful Cotswold village of Bisley where the ancient tradition of dressing the wells continues.

Below: Buckle Street, looking towards Snowshill. (Photograph by Michael Dibb)

The bridge at Bidford-on-Avon with Saxon Fields carpark visible on the right, where in 1921, archaeologists discovered a cunning-woman. (Photograph by Chris J Wood)

One of *Mildyth's* amuletic bucket pendants. (Image copyright The Trustees of the British Museum)

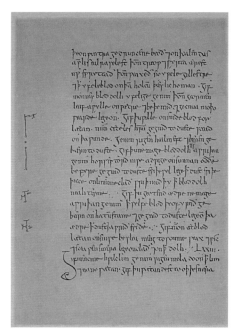

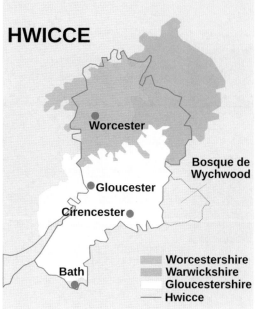

Above left: A page from Bald's *Leechbook* of Old English remedies.

Above right: The *Hwicce* territories. (image by Finn Bjørklid)

Above left: An illustration of Snorri Sturluson from the 1899 edition of Heimskringla.

Above right: The goddess Ēostre/Ostara flies through the heavens, by Johannes Gehrts, 1901.

Above: The silver brooch from Leicestershire with the words 'Wulfgyfe owns me for herself'.

Below: An incomplete example of an Anglo-Saxon large-holed spoon, of the type used for Turning the Riddle.

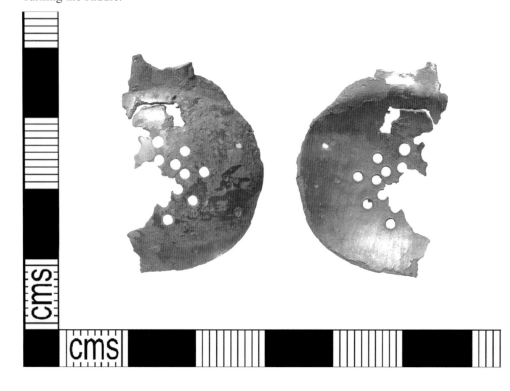

Right: A twelfth century illustration of Woden and his progeny, from *Libellus de primo Saxonum uel Normannorum adventu.*

Below: The goddess Nerthus being paraded on her wagon, by Emil Doepler, 1905.

Above left: The Rollright Stones in the heart of the Cotswolds. Alec Spooner thought the stones were evidence of witchcraft in the murder of Charles Walton. (Photograph by Dennis Turner)

Above right: Clay figurine of Asherah discovered in Judah. (Circa seventh century BCE.)

Below: William Blake's depiction of The Witch of Endor Raising The Spirit of Samuel. (Circa 1800.)

Above: Prüm's Canon *Episcopi*. This copy is circa 1020, and condemns the continued belief that witches can shapeshift and attend Sabbaths.

Right: The entrance to Wayland's Smithy in the Cotswolds.

One of the Bisley wells, located just south from the Church. (Photograph by Mike Baldwin)

Site of the burning of Scotland's last witch Janet Horne. The date is marked as 1722 although it is usually documented as 1727.

An image of Margaret Murray taken in 1928.

Chapter 10

Smoke and Mirrors

'Have you believed or participated in this infidelity, that some wicked women, turned back after Satan, seduced by illusions and phantoms of demons, believe and affirm: that with Diana, a goddess of the pagans, and an unnumbered multitude of women, they ride on certain beasts and traverse many areas of the earth in the stillness of the quiet night, obey her commands as if she were their mistress, and are called on special nights to her service?.. If you have believed these vanities, you shall do penance for two years on the appointed fast days.'

Buchard of Worms, 906

The tenth century Buchard of Worms collected together twenty books, including Regino of Prüm, Abbot of Treves's Canon *Episcopi,* into an organised codex of canon law entitled *Decretum Burchardi.* In its desire to cast pagan traditions and its followers as evil, it unwittingly provides a documented treatise on ancient beliefs that survived into the early medieval period. The above quotation speaks of an ancient tradition that folklorists term the Wild Hunt, where Buchard describes how 'wicked women' who, 'turned back' to the old ways, ride with their goddess through the night sky. The motif of the Wild Hunt appears throughout medieval Church documents and was obviously an enduring belief for common people and an enduring irritation for the Church.

Beyond the Church accounts, the Wild Hunt survives in European myth whereby spectral hunters, led by their deity, traverse the heavens on thundering horses accompanied by howling hounds. The *Anglo-Saxon Chronicle* states:

'...it was seen and heard by many men: many hunters riding. The hunters were black, and great and loathy, and their hounds all black, and wide-eyed and loathy, and they rode on black horses and black he-goats. This was seen in the very deer park in the

81

town of Peterborough, and in all the woods from the same town to
Stamford; and the monks heard the horn blowing that they blew
that night. Truthful men who kept watch at night said that it seemed
to them that there might be about twenty or thirty horn blowers.
This was seen and heard...all through Lenten tide until Easter.'

The identities of these apparitions change depending upon the culture and
time, even finding their way into modern children's minds who believe that
Santa Claus flies through the sky with his entourage of reindeers.

By the eleventh century it was Diana (Artemis in Greek) who ruled
the Yuletide skies over much of Europe, and rampaged with her fearsome
women, chasing wild boar and deer for the winter feasts. With the goddess
taking control of the winter hunt, the people celebrated. The Wild Hunt,
although being supernatural and fearsome, was the harbinger of good
fortune for the coming cold season. Yet as Christianity grew, the hunt
became an ill-fated omen to those who claimed to have witnessed it.

Diana's name comes from the Indo-European root *dyw* meaning day and
this character of light is further confirmed by her Latinised root *diurnal*.
This indicates perhaps, that she was not always associated with the night
and winter, but her identity may have become altered. In Acts 19:35 she is
described as being an image from heaven:

'Men of Ephesus, doesn't everyone know that the city of Ephesus
is guardian of the temple of the great Artemis [Diana] and of her
image, which fell from heaven?'

The famous mythologist and researcher Jacob Grimm in his *Deutsche
Mythologie* of 1835 suggests the Wild Hunt can be traced to a Germanic
origin. This may be the case, although today remnants of the Wild Hunt are
seen to have dispersed throughout Europe making its origins less certain.
In Scandinavia, the hunt was known as the *Oskoreia* or Terrifying Ride and
Odensjakt, Woden's Ride. In Ireland, it is elves that fly the winter skies and
in Orkney the nocturnal riders are fairies.

Walter Map, a priest and courtier to Henry II suggests a British origin
for the hunt. In Britain it was called *Herlaþing* (Herla's Assembly). Herla
is thought to have been a king of the Britons, although the name may have
been a Gaelic version of Woden as Herla has been linked to Herian, one of
Woden's aliases.

Map places Herla in the west of Hwicce country, stating that the Wild
Hunt traverses the boarders of Wales and Herefordshire, resolving in the

River Wye where Herla then disappears into the water. If so, then the tale may contain a further remnant of ancient belief whereby the king is sacrificed in water following his sacred marriage to the goddess and the ingesting of plant seeds. If flying is a forgotten aspect of this sacrificial tradition, then henbane seeds would certainly have had the hallucinatory substance to create an experience of flying. Also, Woden is known to have used 'flying-mead' to aid his supernatural journeys and in Mildþryþ's books we find mention of 'flying-potion'. Map even claims an eyewitness account of the *Herlaþing:*

> 'This household of Herlethingus [Herla's Assembly] was last seen in the marches of Wales and Hereford in the first year of the reign of Henry II, about noonday: they travelled as we do, with carts and sumpter horses, pack-saddles and panniers, hawks and hounds, and a concourse of men and women. Those who saw them first raised the whole country against them with horns and shouts, and ... because they were unable to wring a word from them by addressing them, made ready to extort an answer with their weapons. They, however, rose up into the air and vanished on a sudden.'

Also, in the witch trial of Bessie Dunlop (Chapter 14) she described hearing a tremendous sound of riders rushing past her whilst she was tethering her horse by Restalrig Loch, Scotland. The sound swept past and rushed with 'a hideous rumbling noise' into the deep waters of the lake.

We therefore find preserved in the canon law of Burchard of Worms a description of women flying through the skies on the Yuletide Wild Hunt, just as they had been doing for centuries if not millennia. The inclusion of the words 'wicked women' in the Canon *Episcopi* and Buchard's work is indicative of the timbre of the documents. It is perhaps unsurprising that a new religion should attack the gods of the previous one; this is not uncommon, yet it is the consistent and numerous references to the old religion with its belief in what Tacitus stated to be the essential power of women that is focused upon. For example, the Canon *Episcopi* asks:

> 'Have you believed or participated in this infidelity, that there is any woman who through certain spells and incantations can turn about the minds of men either from hatred to love or from love to hatred? If you have believed or participated in these acts, you shall do penance for one year in the appointed fast days.'

Here is evidence of love magic, showing that finding a suitable spouse, thwarting the attentions of someone undesirable or assuaging loneliness are enduring human concerns. Whereas today we have a number of available sources of help and advice, in ancient times, the local cunning-woman may have been the closest one could find to a counsellor in these matters.

Mildþryþ may well have been called upon to intervene in relationships. We might imagine her listening with compassion to the emotional concerns of a client and then giving advice. As is confirmed in *The Scottish Journal of Healthcare Chaplaincy* (2013), 'Listening is an essential part of caring practice. Being listened to and telling our story is in itself therapeutic and life affirming.' By taking her time to build rapport, listen and thereby create a safe space for her client, Mildþryþ may have enabled emotional disclosure. Add to this some ritualistic and symbolic elements based upon the beliefs of the time and we have a powerful psychological framework for emotional healing. Here is one remedy for love issues from Mildþryþ's repertoire:

'Gif mon sie to unwræne wyl on meolce þa ilcan wyrt, þonne awrænst þu. Wyl on eowe meolce, eft, hindhioloþan, alexandrian, fornetes folm hatte wyrt. Þonne biþ hit swa him leofost bið.'

'If one is not lustful, boil the same plant in milk, then you make that person lustful. Boil in ewe's milk, again, water agrimony, horse parsley and the plant fornets hand, then it will be as if it is dearest to him.'

The combination of plants were believed to interact sympathetically with the desired outcome. For example, water agrimony is usually seen growing in particularly dark, damp places and fornet's hand (wild orchid) is described by Bierbaumer in his 2009 book *Old Names New growth* as having a 'sperm-like, slimy quality of the extracts and the smell of sperm emanating from the testicle shaped bulb enhances the belief'. The sympathetic likenesses here require little further extrapolation. This was an ancient aphrodisiac using like to attract like.

Love spells were used well into recent times although not all use the wholesome ingredients of milk and herbs. Some were designed to over-ride the will of another person:

'Its not this candle alone I stick,
But ....'s heart I mean to prick.
Whether he be asleep or awake,
I'd have him come to me and speak.'

This is not an aphrodisiac designed to restore harmony and sexual desire. This is a summoning spell that seeks to override the will or agency of its victim, and it is recorded in a number of medieval documents as forming the active principle of love spells.

George Bailey of Whimpstone in Hwicce country recounted one example of this spell being used. The item to be pricked is an apple, although in other accounts it is sometimes the shoulder blade of a sheep, which was to be pricked with a knife for nine nights until the desired target arrived. In George's experience, nine nights were not required as the unwitting victim arrived quickly.

George's story recounts that he had been taking supplies to a local woman who claimed that she had special powers and could prove it. The woman said she could summon George's sister to them that very day by sticking twelve new pins into an apple and burning it on the fire whilst chanting. This she did and some hours later his sister arrived. His sister could not say why she had come as the snow was very deep and travel was difficult, but she had not been able to resist the urge.

No spells such as this are found within Mildþryþ's remedies and seem instead to be representative of the darker type of magic that she was sometimes called upon to undo. Although no one was actually harmed during George's encounter with the old woman, there are a number of Mildþryþ's remedies that protect against the dark arts or undo their effects, thus demonstrating that black magic was a very real concern for our ancestors. An account from Yorkshire, for example, describes the essence of the practice:

There was a girl who wished to win back the attention of her lover and used harmful magic to do so. First, she collected together the materials she would need which included a live frog, a box and some pins. She then stabbed the pins into the frog whilst it was alive, being careful to ensure the pins did not cause death, just pain. The wounded frog was then secured in the box and buried in the ground. How long she waited for it to die is unrecorded.

When the frog was dead, the girl extracted a tiny bone from its corpse and secreted it upon her lover so that he would experience the excruciating suffering of the frog, suffering that would only end if he took her back.

This spell demonstrates the intention of black magic which emerges from desires to possess, coerce or control another person through the vehicle of their suffering. Modern psychological analysis might describe such a sorcerer, who seeks control over others by causing them distress as exhibiting a sociopathic personality disorder. This stands in stark contrast to the 'white' magic practiced by those such as Mildþryþ, whose intention was to ease suffering through the divine auspices of her goddess.

Yet by writing his Canon, Prüm was keen to establish in the minds of the common folk that Mildþryþ's abilities were not 'white' magic at all but instead were black magic, inspired by the devil to deceive them. But according to Prüm, the deception went even further – not only was the work of cunning-women diabolically inspired, it did not truly heal anyone at all – its effects were a complete fabrication. Prüm is thus taking a step further than that of Augustine. Where Augustine believed that such women did cause healings to occur, and correctly prophesied the future, Prüm believes this is mistaken. Cunning-women could not heal or foretell the future. The appearance of such things were themselves a deception and therefore unreal.

Prüm used his Canon *Episcopi* to build upon Augustine's foundational re-interpretation of Scripture and the problem of evil. Prüm's work, which influenced Burchard, is the overt piece of Canon Law that led to the witch hysteria of later centuries. It contains features easily recognisable within the later, notorious *Malleus Maleficarum* of 1487 that would inform the structure and philosophy of the witch trials. Yet Prüm's differing interpretation of the reality of women's healing and prophecy caused a dramatic consequence – the evil of diabolical collaboration established by Augustine could now unfold to include the common-folk themselves. Should a person believe in the reality of cunning-women's work and the pagan beliefs underpinning it, then they were no longer an unwitting victim of evil but instead, were actively conspiring with it. Suddenly, anyone who believed they had been healed by a cunning-woman was guilty of evil-doing and so had to undergo punishment and penance.

This altered the locus of accusation towards the common-folk themselves, identifying them as being infidels if they sought the help of cunning-women. Slowly but surely, Mildþryþ's client base was being turned against her.

This is a sophisticated social psychological strategy that has been investigated and exposed by the psychologist Anthony Stahelski. He describes how groups such as religious organisations and cults aim to 'depluralise' people belonging to another group so as to assimilate them into their own. Human beings are a naturally 'pluralised' species. We tend to belong to a number of different groups including family, tribes, cultures and religions. So, to 'depluralise' a person or group involves a strategy with a number of steps including 'self-deindividuation', which means altering a person's relationship to the main symbols, rituals and ideas that formed a person's relationship with their previous group and undermining them. This is then escalated, so that the previous group becomes re-branded as aberrant. Stahelski goes on to explain that the final part of the process is to then dehumanise and demonise the original group and its officers. He warns that this final stage, which aims to establish in the person a total unthinking and unwavering obedience to the new group, can often involve violence.

Prüm's interrogative list aims to cast doubt concerning Mildþryþ's abilities and their source by establishing the unreality of her power and the evil of its genesis. It also seeks to interrogate her prospective patients and punish them if they continue to seek help from her. This ensured that Mildþryþ would be demoted and demonised in the eyes of those she served and re-cast as 'other'.

Chapter 11

Physician to Witch

'Have you done what some women do at the instigation of the devil? When any child has died without baptism, they take the corpse of the little one and place it in some secret place and transfix its little body with a stake, saying that if they did not do so the little child would arise and would injure many? If you have done, or consented to, or believed this, you should do penance for two years on the appointed days.'

Prüm, Canon Episcopi

The above quotation is typical of the list of questions that demonise cunning-women whilst putting fear and doubt in the hearts of those seeking their help. Like many of the questions, this one exposes the pagan traditions that the clergy were seeking to obliterate, in this case, some of the beliefs surrounding 'deviant' burials.

Mortality rates in newborns and those born prematurely were terribly high and often parents were not able to have their child baptised before death. In the Early Middle Ages, the Church taught parents that their unbaptised infants would spend their eternity in perdition along with murderers and other sinners, and this new belief caused great anxiety and elevated grief.

Yet parents were caught between two worlds – their ancient beliefs taught them that in situations where the infant's soul was at risk, or posed a risk, then a stake through the heart was one remedy that could ensure their peaceful rest. By making this old ritualistic tradition into something abhorrent, parents were consequently left confused, fearful and bereft.

In another entry from the canon we find a further belief adhered to by women. It concerns those mothers who were unfortunate enough to die in childbirth along with their child:

'Have you done what some women, filled with the boldness of the devil are wont to do? When some woman is to bear a child and is not able, if when she cannot bear it she dies in her pangs, they transfix the mother and the child in the same grave with a stake, driven into the earth. If you have done or consented to this, you should do penance for two years on the appointed days.'

In their 2011 article for the *Current Archaeology* magazine, Sayer, Mortimer and Simpson reported on their discoveries in the Oakington Anglo-Saxon cemetery; they found 'a pregnant woman buried with a rich array of grave goods on the margins of a large early Anglo-Saxon cemetery (that) provided new insights into female fertility, pregnancy and the life course.'

Nicknamed 'Queeny' by the archaeological team due to her obvious wealth, this woman was buried with the bones of a baby straddling her abdomen indicating a transverse pregnancy. Queeny therefore died from a condition that would today be remedied by caesarean section.

Despite her obvious status and the careful, respectful way Queeny was interred, the researchers observed some surprising features that marked her burial as deviant. Having died during or just following childbirth, she was placed at the far edge of the cemetery, as was Mildþryþ, with the east-west orientation of her corpse leading the archeologists to conclude her 'death was treated with suspicion, leaving her branded polluted'. Further graves of pregnant women have been discovered with similarly deviant motifs.

Within some graves it seems clear that the foetus was expelled from the birthing canal after the mother's death. This strange, and rather macabre situation is known today as 'coffin birth' and this post-mortem delivery can occur after the body of the mother has been buried. It happens because of a build-up of gases due to the putrefaction process. These gases would cause pressure in the abdominal cavity and push the foetus from the womb after the death of the mother. If the early Anglo-Saxons or Britons had noticed this phenomenon, then it is possible a superstition would have arisen in relation to this unfortunate occurrence.

Mildþryþ's healing books contain extensive and often elaborate remedies and prescriptions surrounding fertility, conception, pregnancy and childbirth. From advice such as the avoidance of vigorous horse riding to the altogether bizarre recommendation to jump over dead men's graves, issues surrounding childbirth were of a great concern for women. Mildþryþ, as the community physician, would have been responsible for this difficult and life threatening process and when things went wrong, her spiritual knowledge would have informed the inhumation and any supernatural adherences necessary. The person recommending that stakes be thrust through the bodies of mothers who died in childbirth, or the infant not yet baptised, would have been the physician/priest of the day, doing her best to ensure both mother and child rested peacefully.

We may therefore be able to say with increasing confidence that the 'women' continuously referred to in the Canon *Epsicopi* and the later *Malleus* are cunning-women such as Mildþryþ and her later colleagues, as this next excerpt further indicates:

> 'Have you collected medicinal herbs with evil incantations, not with the creed and the Lord's prayer, that is with the singing of the "credo in Deum" and the paternoster?'

This question exposes something of a paradoxical issue for the Church; on the one hand, medicine was a necessity and so the collection of herbs could not be outlawed, yet as medical practice had an established lineage of female pagan practice, something had to be done nonetheless. So it was necessary to retain the harvesting of herbs and the knowledge that went with it, whilst striking at the heart of the traditions and gender that had been responsible for it. *Bald's Leechbook III* and *Lacnunga* may have been commissioned to retain the knowledge of the cunning-women before their role completely disappeared.

The monasteries therefore appropriated and preserved Mildþryþ's remedies yet added new wording such as the 'credo in Deum' in place of earlier pagan invocations interpreted by the clergy as 'evil incantations'. This Christianisation of pagan content is evident within many of the old remedies as this cure from the *Lacnunga* manuscript shows:

> 'Gif se wyrm sy nyþergewend oððe se bledenda fic, bedelf ænne wrid cileþenigan moran ond nim mid þinum twam handum uppeweardes ond sing þærofer viiii paternostra, æt þam nigeðan æt libera nos a malo, bred hy þonne up, ond nim of þam ciðe ond of oþrum þæt þær sy an lytel cuppe ful, ond drenc hy þonne ond beðige hine mon to wearman fyre, him bið sona sel.'

> *'If a worm is turned downwards or a bleeding haemorrhoid, dig round a clump of celandine roots and take them with your two upturned hands and sing nine paternosters over them, then at the ninth, at 'deliver us from evil' pull it up, and take off the shoot and others that might be there, one small cup full and then immerse them and let him warm himself by a fire, soon he will be better.'*

Anglo-Saxon scholars John Grattan and Charles Singer believe that the 'worm' that is 'turned downwards' is describing an anal fissure. Yet a more accurate translation of *bledenda fic* (bleeding fig) would be haemorrhoids. The remedy calls for the use of celandine, which has a rich medical history – due to its acrid nature it has been used to treat many skin conditions such as eczema, warts and even opaqueness of the cornea. The final part of this remedy is unclear, as we do not know for sure whether the plant is to be applied topically to the piles or drunk as a tonic. If the latter, then little benefit would be found. As a poultice, then celandine root would possibly work, although the process would be rather painful.

Remnants of a larger healing ritual are evident here, as the plant must be harvested in a precise way. Digging round the root, taking it in upturned hands whilst singing nine adjurations and then pulling the root from the ground on the ninth alone, indicates superstition. The animistic worldview of pagan belief saw plants as embodying spirit, and spirits required respect and recompense for what was taken from them. To slight a spirit would be to invite its revenge in the form of disharmony or illness. Harvesting a plant was therefore a serious act that required care and reverence.

Using the number nine was one way of ensuring respect and divine intervention for the plant. The number had great significance for the Anglo-Saxons as it symbolised the three faces of the goddess known sometimes as the Norns or Fates. Although paganism is typified by a plurality of gods, the esoteric meaning of this plurality has been misinterpreted in the last few centuries. Similarly to the trinity of the Father, Son and Holy Spirit, pagan goddesses were often a singular deity expressed through three principles.

Of the continued reverence towards the Fates, the Canon enquires:

> 'Have you done as some women are wont to do at certain times of the year? That is, have you prepared the table in your house and set on the table your food and drink, with three knives, that if those three sisters whom past generations and old-time foolishness called the Fates should come they may take refreshment there,'

The Fates are here demoted as 'old-time foolishness' within the continuing process of demonization as identified by the psychologist Stahelski. Those who continue to respect cunning-women and follow their advice and traditions at 'certain times of the year' are now held in suspicion for lingering adherence to the old 'other' group.

Prüm's Canon *Episcopi,* which informed the writing of Buchard of Worms, stands temporally equidistant between Augustine's Scriptural interpretations and the *Malleus Maleficarum*. It is one of the first documents to overtly demonstrate the process of demonization whereby female physicians became the medieval witch, yet why the term 'witch' evolved from the name of the Hwicce tribe is yet to be answered.

'Witch' is a powerful word. 'Ding dong, the wicked witch is dead' isn't the most usual obituary for a woman dying in the twenty-first century. Yet this was the sentiment of many upon the death of Margaret Thatcher in 2013 whose lives had been negatively impacted by her policies.

Two years earlier on the other side of the globe, Australia's Prime Minister Julia Gillard was similarly labelled a witch. Slogans on placards appeared on the news stating 'Ditch the Witch' along with silhouettes of a grizzled old crone flying upon a broom. Not all female leaders are called a witch of course (and often male leaders are depicted as devils), but when emotions run high, or the woman concerned is particularly controversial, 'Witch' is often the go-to word.

During an interview, Gillard described how misogynist statements soon followed the label of 'witch'. Sexist cartoons circulated stating she had 'small breasts, huge thighs and a big red box'. She had hoped, she said, that it would all just die down and furthermore; she was concerned that if she reacted then she would be labelled hysterical too.

The American psychiatrist Thomas Szasz contends that the label of 'hysteric' took the place of the word 'witch' during the late nineteenth century when women who did not conform to 'normal' behaviours, whether they practiced magic or not, could no longer be tortured, tried and killed, but instead could be incarcerated in asylums. Szasz notes that measures of what constituted admittance as an hysteric are remarkably similar to those used to accuse earlier women of witchcraft.

Yet it was only just before the completing of Prüm's Canon *Episcopi* that we begin to see the Old English word *wicce* being generally used to describe cunning-women. *Wicce*, having dropped the Germanic prefix of *h*, (and so drawing closer to the Middle English *wiche* that would become our modern word witch) appears for the first time during the reign of King Alfred. Before this, in 603 for example, Bede refers to the Hwicce as a British Christian tribe, retaining their Christianity from the Roman occupation and therefore being distinct from the Augustinian form of Christianity that had taken root in Canterbury. Yet archaeology does not necessarily support this view as Mildþryþ and her community display marked Saxon features. Also a record from the *Anglo-Saxon Chronicle* dated 577 states:

> 'Here Cuthwine and Ceawil fought against the Britons and they killed three kings, Coinmagil and Candidn and Fairnmagil, in the

place which is called Dyrham; and took three cities. Gloucester and Cirencester and Bath.'

The date of the Battle of Dyrham (Deorham) is current with Mildþryþ's life and indicates this West Saxon victory as the point where the Dobunnic tribe of Britons gave way to the Saxon tribe of Hwicce. So Bede may have been partially correct; the Hwicce may have been early Saxon settlers who merged with, albeit forcibly, the British Dobunnic tribe.

In 628, following the Battle of Cirencester, the Hwicce became a sub-kingdom of the central Anglo-Saxon kingdom of Mercia. Known also as the Hwiccians, they were viewed as a distinct and semi-autonomous tribe as the founding of a Bishop's See in Worcester in 680 evidences. The See was used to identify groups who were considered to be distinct. The Bishops of Worcester even bore the title *Episcopus Hwicciorum – Hwicciorum* being the Latinised version of Hwicce.

In 740 Adelred, a Hwicce governor gave lands in Barton to the Monastery of Gloucester, and in a Royal charter of 780 we find the entire area of the Cotswolds termed *Hwicciorum*. By 811 the Mercian king Kenulph confirmed that the Hwicce, also termed in a local dialect as Wixes, had given lands to the Church. It is also around this time that Royal charters begin to fully Anglicise the Hwicce as Wicce.

It would be almost three hundred years following Augustine of Canterbury's meeting beneath the oak tree on the edge of Hwicce land that we find their name becoming identified with magical practices. Before this, there were a number of words the Anglo-Saxons used to describe those working with magic, herbs and prophecy:

Drýmann- sorcerer
Drýicge- sorceress
Egesgríme- sorceress
Hægtes- a pythoness
Helrýnegu- a female black magician
Galdere- enchanter or diviner
Lyblæca- wizard
Scinnlæca- necromancer
Wælcyrge- divine woman
Hellrúna- black magician
Láca- magical necromancer
Scinnlæce- woman magical healer

Wyrtgælstre- woman who works with herbs
Leódrúne- a cunning woman

This is by no means a comprehensive list. There were many terms used to describe people working in magical ways indicating the great importance that supernatural concerns held. Today, we might use witch, magician and sorcerer but we do not retain the complexity of nuances for this type of practice.

It is within the Laws of *Ælfred,* written in about 890 that we find the plural for *wicce*, which is *wiccan*, being used alongside the terms enchanter and sorceress. Alfred's use of the word marks the first recorded instance of the tribal name being associated with magical practice:

'Tha faemnan, the gewuniath onfon gealdorcraeftigan and scinlaecan and wiccan, ne laet thu tha libban.'

'Women who are accustomed to receiving enchanters and sorceresses and witches, do not let them live.'

Ælfred's statement is similar to the infamous passage in Exodus 22:18 – 'Thou shalt not suffer a witch to live'. This phrase has caused much debate and continues to inform prejudice against witches today. The translation of the Hebrew *mekashaph* in Exodus 22:18, is contested and is often cited as a mistranslation that fuelled the witch craze:

'This quote, found in the King James Version of the Bible, has been widely held responsible for the witch burnings that plagued Europe, and later America, in the Early Modern Period (1450 C.E. – 1750 C.E.). But the murderous practice may have all been the result of a Biblical mistranslation.'
(Elizabeth Sloane, Haaretz, 2017.)

Two mistranslations have been put forward; first, biblical scholar Kenneth Kitchen has suggested the word *mekashaph* comes from the root of the verb 'to cut'. Combined with the fact that in Deuteronomy 18:9-10 *mekashaph* is included in a general list of evil practices such as sorcery and necromancy, this has led some scholars to argue that the actual translation is 'poisoner' – specifically, a person who cuts up plants to poison others. Another biblical scholar, Merrill F. Unger, contends, however, that the root is 'to mutter', and so describes a sorcerer using incantations.

Although it is popularly held that the King James Bible (commissioned in 1604) was the first to use the term witch in relation to murder, the 890 quotation from Alfred might suggest the notion was already in existence, albeit the murder of women seeking the assistance of cunning-women.

Alfred may have equated *wicce* with evil magic-workers to forward his own political agenda concerning Mercia, where the Hwicce were still a powerful, semi-independent tribe. 'Mercia' itself comes from the Old English *Miercna rice* meaning boundary folk and it is well known that parts of Mercia resisted Christianity well into the seventh century. The first Mercian king, Penda, was a pagan, and he may be the final clue to solve the mystery of how a tribal name became used to describe what was to become the evil embodiment of the witch. In the *Anglo-Saxon Chronicle* it states:

'Penda was Pybba's offspring, Pybba was Cryda's offspring, Cryda Cynewald's offspring, Cynewald Cnebba's offspring, Cnebba Icel's offspring, Icel Eomer's offspring, Eomer Angeltheow's offspring, Angeltheow Offa's offspring, Offa Wermund's offspring, Wermund Wihtlæg's offspring, Wihtlæg Woden's offspring.'

Penda was known, even by the ninth century when the Chronicle was written in the court of King Alfred, as the descendant of Woden. The chronicle also states that Penda ruled from 626 for thirty years and succeeded in many battles including those against what was to become Alfred's Wessex, which was once the southern area of Hwicce territory. This means that the Gregorian attempts to convert the Hwicce in 603 were not entirely successful and it is likely that King Alfred, a Christian with a dream of uniting England, saw Penda's old tribe with its continuation of pagan adherences as a problem. Alfred was also dealing with Viking invasions and believed this new terror was occurring due to the un-godly pagan practices of the British people.

Some researchers such as Frank Stenton have forwarded the theory that the Hwicce were a sub-kingdom specifically formed by Penda, as no mention of them precedes him and their name first occurs during his reign or close after. This cannot be verified but may provide an explanation as to why their name became used by Alfred to identify what he would have viewed as the heretical pagan practices of women using magic, herbs and prophesy. Indeed, by the fifteenth century the infamous *Malleus Maleficarum* states of the term 'witch':

'of all superstition it is essentially the vilest, the most evil and the worst, wherefore it derives its name from doing evil, and from blaspheming the true faith'.

The historian Nicholas Higham wrote that when Penda died 'his destruction sounded the death-knell of English paganism as a political ideology and public religion.' So if the Hwicce were Penda's creation, loyal to the line of Woden, this may have marked them out as subversive and problematic.

Mercia was one of the last pagan strongholds to fall to Christianity following Penda's death, yet it is unlikely this conversion went smoothly. Continued adherence to pagan practices surrounding the value of women in magico-medical healing practices would have marked them out, perhaps causing Alfred to use their very name to identify such traditions.

It may thus be possible to isolate the late ninth century as the time when the Hwicce tribe's title became equated with what we call witchcraft. Alfred was certainly using the term this way in 890, yet in neighbouring Mercia, Lord Ethelred (881-911) appoints Osree, descendent of Penda, as a governor of the Wicce, indicating that in Mercia, the meaning of Wicce was yet to be altered. So this may have been a transitional time. There is even evidence that during Alfred's reign, previous documents were altered to include the new usage of the word *wicce*.

In Halitgar's ninth century *Latin Penitential* for example, he laments at the continued stupidity of common folk who place offerings at sacred pagan sites or seek healing at them. He specifies that people do these things because it is what 'the witches teach':

> 'Some men are so blind that they bring their offering to earth-fast stone and also to trees and to wellsprings, as the witches teach *[swa wiccan tæcaþ]*, and are unwilling to understand how stupidly they do or how that dead stone or that dumb tree might help them or give forth health when they themselves are never able to stir from their place.'

According to historian Rob Means, Halitgar wrote his *Penitential* around 820, pre-dating Alfred's use of the word *wicce* as witch. Yet David Petterson has discovered that the phrase *swa wiccan tæcaþ* (as the witches teach) is a later addition to Halitgar's text, occurring when his writings were translated from Latin into Old English during Alfred's reign.

By the tenth century, we find Alfred's usage commonplace. In *Ælfric* of Eynesham's homilies for example, the word *wiccan* is used exclusively as a description for those who are consulted for prophesy:

> 'Ne sceal se cristena befrinan tha fulan wiccan be his gesundfulnysse.'

> *'A Christian should not consult foul witches concerning his prosperity.'*

In The Witan of King Ethelred, 975-979, the words *wicce* and *wiccan* are firmly established and used along with necromancers, perjurers and whores:

> 'And if witches (*wiccan*) or soothsayers, magicians or whores, necromancers or perjurers be anywhere found in the country, let them diligently be driven out of this country, and this people be purified,'

In just one hundred years since Alfred's first overt use of the Hwicce's name to describe sorcery, it had been successfully adopted as a label for diabolical magic. From now onwards, wicce means a practitioner of witchcraft, which no longer includes anything beneficial - forever identifying Mildþryþ and her activities of healing, magic and prophesy with malevolent practitioners of black magic.

Chapter 12

Sacred Space and Christian Magic

'It is ordered that persons who both eat of a feast in the abominable places of the pagans and carry food... and eat it subject themselves to a penance of two years.'

Halitgar's Penitential, 820

'Every priest zealously promote Christianity, and totally extinguish every heathenism and forbid well-worshippings...and the vain practices which are carried on with various spells, and with sacred spots, and with elders, and also with various other trees, and with stones, and with many various delusions,'.

King Edgar, 958-979

Two hundred years before Alfred succeeded in creating witches, Britain was already causing quite the scandal in Rome. In a letter to Abbot Mellitus, first Saxon Bishop of London, Pope Gregory referred to his 'deliberation on the affair of the English'. The affair referred to the persistent, rampant paganism that just wouldn't desist as it had done, to a large degree in the rest of Europe. Britain was a problem and the Pope had an idea:

> 'To his most beloved son, the Abbot Mellitus ... upon mature deliberation on the affair of the English, determined upon that the temples of the idols in that nation ought not to be destroyed; but let the idols that are in them be destroyed; let holy water be made and sprinkled in the said temples, let altars be erected, and relics placed.
>
> 'For if those temples are well built, it is requisite that they be converted from the worship of devils to the service of the true God; that the nation, seeing that their temples are not destroyed, may remove error from their hearts, and knowing and adoring the true God, may the more familiarly resort to the places to which they have been accustomed ... For there is no doubt that it is impossible to efface everything at once from their obdurate minds.'

Pope Gregory had identified the importance of sacred spaces and places in the hearts and minds of the common people. His statement that the English 'may the more familiarly resort to the places to which they have been accustomed', shows an understanding of the power of familiar practices in sacred spaces. This remains true today as spaces like homes, gardens, parks and community areas provide important points of navigation during our daily lives – they map our routines and define our structures of work, rest and time with family and friends. When a beloved haunt is knocked down or altered it can be an emotional event. A new place must be found to fill the gap and keep the map of our lives coherent and stable. Traditions, routines and beliefs mingle with these spaces. As archaeologist Kathryn Reese-Taylor explains, 'sacred landscapes are religious and philosophical touchstones, as well as powerful socio-political statements.'

Forcible conversion, which was working reasonably well throughout much of Europe was less successful in Britain and so Gregory, building upon the theological and intellectual foundations laid by Augustine, turned to a more solid form of appropriation – he would turn the old pagan temples and sacred spaces into Christian ones.

Seeds of old memories regarding this appropriation of time and space can be found peppering the later witch trials. Locations mentioned in trial transcripts can be very specific and are often described as places where spirits and fairies meet and converse with the mortals of this world. These liminal spaces abound with powerful, mythic meaning and as Donald McIlmichall poignantly describes, offer an 'oral narrative map of landscape touched everywhere by footprints of the supernatural'.

It is important to note that by the time of the trials, most of which occurred between the fourteenth to seventeenth centuries, the devil and his minions were now fully accepted as the source of otherworldly knowledge and supernatural communication outside of the Church. Pagan cosmology and devil worship were established as symbiotic, and this notion existed as a reality in the psyche of the clergy and much of the population.

In 1514, centuries after Mildþryþ's death, two individuals from Somerset (the old southern area of Hwicce country) were accused of witchcraft. Specifically, they were named as two of those who continued an ancient practice known as 'Mendepe.' It remains unclear exactly what the accusation of 'Mendepe' is, but John Panter and his wife (or sister) Agnes Panter were said to visit a site on the local Mendip Hills every year on the Eve of St John to converse with demons.

The Eve of Saint John commemorates the birth of John the Baptist and thanks to Pope Gregory; the feast day remains ritualistically similar to its host festival of Litha, the summer solstice, which was celebrated with fires. John and Agnes lived in the village of Doulting, close to Glastonbury with its myths of King Arthur, and Wookey Hole and its tale of a witch turned to stone, all of which nestle close to the Mendip Hills. The tradition of 'Mendepe' for which the couple was accused is certainly linked to this ancient landscape.

High ground like the Mendip Hills, so often marked by Bronze Age barrows and Iron Age burial mounds, feature in many witch trial accounts: for example, Isabel Haldeane who stood accused in Perth, 1623, described how fairies lived in sacred hills. In Isobel Gowdie's trial of 1664, the accused spoke of taking trips to a 'Fairy Hill' to enter into communication with spirits.

To the north east of the Cotswolds are the Dunstable Downs, where a number of Bronze Age burial mounds called the Knolls can be found. Like the Mendips, it is high, impressive terrain marked by ancient sites. In 1667, Elizabeth Pratt accused three women from Dunstable of meeting together at the Three Knolls there to bewitch the children of Thomas Heyward. She said that 'the devil appeared to her about a fortnight since in the form of a catt, and commanded her to goe to those three persons aforesaid to seeke the destroying of the two children…'. Elizabeth went on to describe two meetings that took place at the Knolls where she accompanied the so-called witches who put a curse on 'the eldest childe of the said Heyward, that they had two meetings about it whereof one was at the Three Knolls upon the Dunstable Downes, and the other a little lower upon the said Downes.'

It is unlikely that the women truly cursed Heyward's children. By 1667, the witch hysteria was in full swing and most people had a good idea of the measures of guilt and requirements for accusation. The cry of 'witch' became a useful way for simply getting other people into trouble and seeking revenge for personal slights.

Ancient Hwicce country is even now teeming with some of the most magnificent ancient sites in Britain. It is here that you will find the stone circles of Stonehenge, Avebury and the Rollrights. Here also is the mysterious hill of Silbury as well as the long barrow of Wayland's Smithy and many further monuments. Wychwood, (or *Hwiccewudu* in Old English), is said to be the most haunted forest in England – Charbury village website describes it as having been known for its 'riotous Forest Fairs' such as the

Whitsun Feast that ran until 1827 when a local clergyman had the event stopped due to what he termed 'gross improprieties'.

In 963 another clergyman took great exception to the local people's continued persistence for honouring the springs and wells. A particular well in the middle of Wychwood seemed to attract the habit, as it was known for its healing properties. Similarly to the Bisley well traditions that were re-introduced by Reverend Kemble, the custom survives and locals still attend the well to create a healing elixir from the water. The groups who keep this practice alive say it is an ancient Celtic ritual.

Visitors today can still walk through Wychwood and visit the healing spring at Lady Well. Passing through Ascot-under-Wychwood and Shipton-under-Wychwood, Wychwood itself lies just south east from Bidford-on-Avon.

The Hwicce, it seems, did not give over their sacred spaces as easily as those in the rest of Britain. Indeed, as Stephen Yeates discovered, the Hwicce experienced 'stable communal development into the fifth and sixth centuries AD' which created a confident and secure tribal structure with strongly held beliefs.

The famous Neolithic long barrow of Wayland's Smithy named after Wayland the Smith, exemplifies just how much pagan sites, traditions and beliefs retained value during the conversion times in Hwicce territory and how gods, goddesses and their heroic tales informed the landscape. Wayland was a Teutonic god mentioned in Beowulf and worshipped throughout Germania, Scandinavia and Anglo-Saxon England. He was son of the giant Wade, who had shrines across the North of England, although Wade's Barrow (*Weardaes Beorh*) is nearby the Smithy. The first written record of *Welandes Smithan* is in a Saxon boundary charter for Compton Beauchamp dated 955. In art, Wayland appears alongside the three Norns on the Franks Casket, an eighth century Anglo-Saxon whalebone box from Northumbria. In the heart of Hwicce territory, Weyland has been thought to be a pseudonym for Woden.

Names can be revealing. Pagan's Hill for example, indicates a continuation of old beliefs and the river Wye (*wēoh* meaning idol) that slices through the borders of Hwicce country is thought to have evolved from the Celtic *uogia* meaning wagon. Combined with the tale of King Herla ending his Wild Hunt in the waters of the Wye, this translation lends credence to the theory of an early tradition of goddess worship in the area, where the goddess is paraded in her wagon before joining with a consort who is later sacrificed in the river with a belly full of seeds.

By the tenth century, churches were being constructed of stone upon earlier pagan sites. A good example can be found in Bisley village where, during an excavation in 1861, fragments of two pagan altars were found beneath the church tower. In the nearby village of Ozelworth, the church stands in the centre of an ancient stone circle – although the stones are long gone and probably form part of the church's foundations. Then there is the church of Daglingworth where the words *Dea Metres* are inscribed into its Saxon wall. *Dea Metres* was the Romano-British name for the Triune goddess once worshipped on the site before the church was constructed.

Churches often obscure earlier pagan sites. Look closely at many parish buildings and you can often see evidence of mounds or ditches denoting the structures of previous times. Yet it was more difficult to disguise or alter natural structures of the landscape such as wells and springs and here we find retained marked pagan practices such as the well dressing ceremony of Bisley. Bisley retains seven of its pagan wells. In one, nicknamed the 'Bonehouse,' the body of a priest was found dead. The story goes that the priest was called out one night to attend a dying parishioner yet when he failed to arrive as expected a search was organised and his body was discovered at the bottom of the well. The date of the event is unknown but the memorial to him that sits above the well is twelfth century.

Another story concerns the 'Bisley Boy'. In the nineteenth century, whilst working on the foundation of the new school, workmen discovered a stone coffin containing the body of a young girl. The vicar, Thomas Keble, apparently confessed that a terrible conspiracy had been hidden by one of his predecessors – during the reign of Henry VIII, the King's daughter Princess Elizabeth had once stayed at Over Court in Bisley. Unfortunately, the princess died whilst there and the villagers and priest were so scared of incurring Henry's anger that they decided to replace the princess with an imposter. The only likeness they could find, however, was actually a boy. As the boy grew up he could never marry as this would reveal the deception, and so he became the Virgin Queen.

In the Cotswolds alone, there are over twenty sacred wells or springs still in existence. Our Lady's Well, Hampstead, stands beside an old Iron Age earthwork and is approached by a small path leading from the churchyard. A structure surrounds the spring and on its eastern side is a worn relief depicting three figures. Although the local historian Canon W. Bazeley suggests it may represent St Anne standing between her daughter St Mary and an angel, it is also possible that the name Anne was adopted for the site from the similarly sounding Waan, an old West Saxon version of the name Woden. The well is known for its healing properties.

Another Our Lady's Well can be found to the east of Lower Swell village. Just off from the A436 is a public right of way and the small well is to the right of the driveway to Abbotswood. A nearby standing stone called the Hoar Stone (also horestone), once part of a Neolithic burial chamber is said to come alive at midnight and drink from the well. The word hoar describes frost. A hoarfrost means a frost forming as greyish white tendrils, like an old man's beard. It's from the Old English *'har'*, meaning grey and venerable.

A further well associated with healing properties lies between the river Avon and the B4040 at Luckington, just as the road moves north towards Sherston. It's known as Hancock's Well and is described by John Aubrey as being:

> 'so extremely cold that in summer one cannot long endure one's hand in it. It does much good to the eies. It cures the itch, etc. By precipitation it yields a white sediment, inclining to yellow like a kind of fine flour. I believe it is much impregnated with nitre.'

Pope Gregory's campaign to appropriate pagan temple sites and construct churches upon them was highly successful, with a handful of notable exceptions, particularly in Hwicce country. Yet when it came to sacred wells, these were often hidden in remote fields or woodlands and so it was more difficult to alter these sites in a meaningful way. Rededication therefore served to aid the project, and wells and springs became the sites of saints and characters from the Christian story in place of the old deities. This enabled a continuation of generally unaltered engagement with these sacred spaces, with the old ways surviving under the cloak of leaved canopies and midnight skies. Rivers and other landmarks such as hills and ravines also became re-named and dedicated to new characters.

Kathryn Reese-Taylor has discovered that ancient sacred landscapes are often constructed from 'features separated by large distances, woven together into a sacred landscape that covers many square kilometres,' forming a sophisticated and culturally important site. She was talking about a recently excavated site in the Basin of Mexico yet this seems true for many ancient religious sites across the world. Hwicce country is no exception and recently, new archaeological evidence from the area around Stonehenge is revealing a network of features more extensive than previously known.

The iconic Saracen stones of Stonehenge are in fact the most recent additions to a more ancient and extensive construction.

Pope Gregory's ambition to assimilate paganism ironically preserved it beneath the umbrella of Catholicism. Eostre was alive and well in her role of spring goddess with her new consort and sacrificial mate, Jesus. Catholic Saints had assumed the positions of old gods honoured at ancient wells, and remedies and charms were being performed with the tag-on of the Credo, Paternoster and a few saints' names. With some minor tweaks here and there, paganism was continuing with a Christian flavour. As Emma Wilby describes:

> 'There is no doubt that allegiance to nature spirits and pagan deities masqueraded behind the worship of the saints; that ancient traditions of ancestor worship lay at the core of the cult of the dead and that the most sacred events in the Christian calendar, such as Christmas and Easter, were superimposed over already-existing pre-Christian festivals.'

By the time of the witch trials, most of the pagan gods and invocations had been successfully replaced by Christian themes, but the traditions remained. A healing charm from 1623 shows how an old remedy for all types of fever has been successfully altered to fit into an acceptable Christian mould:

> 'The quaquand fever and the trembling fever,
> And the sea fever and the land fever,
> Bot as the head fever and the hart fever,
> And all the fevers that God creatit.
> In Sanct Johnes name, Sanct Peteris name,
> And all the sanct of heavin's name,
> Our lord Jesus Chrystis name.'

Yet all was not well. Emergent denominations had noticed the lingering paganism beneath the Catholic exterior. For example, objects of the Catholic Mass had assumed magical significance with cunning-women turning away from traditional amulets such as the rabbit's foot and English mandrake and substituting instead objects such as communion wafers, reliquary items and holy water. These items, just like the pre-Christian ones, were ascribed inherent magical power. There is even evidence that Catholic priests consulted cunning-women as this account preserved by Joseph Train in his 1814 *Strains of the Mountain Muse* indicates:

'I am acquainted myself with a … clergyman who actually procured from a person who pretended to skill in charms two small pieces of carved wood, to be kept in his father's cow-house as a security for the health of his cows.'

Following Sunday communion, priests turned a blind eye to those of their congregation who had only pretended to eat the communion wafer. Many parishioners would give a show of taking and eating when in fact they had already slipped it from their hands and secreted it within the folds of their garments. Communion wafers were thought to have strong magical properties and so people would take them home, crush them up and sprinkle the crumbs around home and hearth to protect the family, just as they had done in former times with sacred cakes from the pagan feasts.

Catholicism and paganism used each other. Almost every aspect of the Catholic faith in Britain and to a lesser degree, other parts of Northern Europe assimilating earlier pagan traditions, yet once assimilated, paganism in turn utilised the Catholic faith as a host for its own continuance. As Keith Thomas explains, Catholicism brought 'an organized system of magic designed to bring supernatural remedies to bear upon earthly problems'. It's even told that a cunning-woman from Orkney performed healing by simply holding the leaf of a herb between her thumb and forefinger and whilst rubbing it reciting, '*In nomine patris filii et spiritus sancti.*' It was in this light that the protestant puritans viewed the 'old faith' of Catholicism.

Before the reformation, which began some time before Martin Luther formally rejected Catholic practices, witches (for this is what they were now called) were relatively safe from extreme persecution as long as they did not cause any harm. Some distinctions were therefore still apparent between good or evil uses for witchcraft, although this would change radically following the publication of the *Malleus Maleficarum* and the fall of Catholicism in Britain. As Lizanne Henderson notes:

'The protestant reinvention of a world in which there could only be the forces of good and evil, while undoubtedly well-intended, effectively shattered the grey area once inhabited by witches, charmers and a host of magical beings, consigning them all to the ranks of the Devil, whose power appeared to be growing stronger than ever.'

Rumblings of reformation were first felt in 1527 when Henry VIII made a request of Pope Clement VII that his marriage to Catherine of Aragon be annulled. Yet when the Pope, who had previously given Henry permission to marry Catherine (the widow of his brother Arthur), did not agree, Henry remained determined and set in motion a series of events that would eventually lead to a break with the Church of Rome and the demise of Papal authority in England.

Catholicism would be rooted out and its powers passed from the Pope to the Crown. Many reformist documents can be found worrying about how 'the whole body of the common people [are] popishly addicted'. Yet this addiction was complex as it was also noticed that this popish obsession obscured the fact that people had little understanding of Christianity itself, and saw it as no more than a changing vocabulary superimposed upon earlier practices.

The reformist Bishop Stephen Gardiner for example, lamented the lack of impact that Christianity had on the immediacy of people's lives. Whilst visiting a number of country parishes he encountered problems; in a Cambridgeshire church for example, he observed that following the sermon people would simply get up and leave, going 'straight out of the church, home to drink'. In the same parish, he also witnessed the forcible removal of a man due to his 'most loathsome farting'.

This attitude of disrespect was examined and it was found, in the words of John Jewel, Bishop of Salisbury, that when it came to the common people 'they know not what the scriptures are; they know not that there are any scriptures'. The English clergyman Nicholas Bownde further complained in 1606 that people still did not understand Scripture, the stories being 'as strange unto them as any news that you can tell them'. A year later John Norden discovered that people often lived 'far from any church or chapel, and are as ignorant of God or of any civil course of life as the very savages among the infidels'. Both Jewel and Norden made their observations in the heart of ancient Hwicce country.

Deep within the countryside of Britain, it seems many people had been simply going through the motions of Christianity. They attended Church because they had to. They stood, knelt, recited and crossed when, where and because they had to. Yet the theology, philosophy and dogma were mostly lost within the toil and trials of a harsh daily life in a country that had its own, indigenous stories to tell.

The increasing limitations on clerical powers were evident in Henry's Witchcraft Act of 1542. There had been a right for accused witches known as 'benefit of the clergy' whereby the accused might be spared the death penalty if they could read a scriptural verse. This right was revoked, and although repealed in 1547, it surfaced again in the Witchcraft Act of 1604. The Act of 1542 introduced serious penalties for anyone who:

> 'practised or exercised, any Invovacons or cojuracons of Sprites witchecraftes enchauntementes or sorceries to thentent to fynde money or treasure or to waste consume or destroy any persone in his bodie membres, or to pvoke [provoke] any persone to unlawfull love, or for any other unlawfull intente or purpose ... or for dispite of Cryste, or for lucre of money, dygge up or pull downe any Crosse or Crosses or by such Invovacons or cojuracons of Sprites witchecraftes enchauntementes or sorceries or any of them take upon them to tell or declare where goodes stollen or lost shall become.'

The punishment for any of these crimes was death and the forfeiture of property and possessions. This had the consequence that the family of an accused witch was left destitute, similarly to the families of heretics during the Catholic extermination of the Cathars. It also completely collapsed any remnant of distinction between white and black magic that had clung on with some hope, so that any practice using ancient places or belief structures was now seen as wholly malevolent.

Yet where witchcraft had once been an accusation against cunning-women and as time progressed, any woman or man seen as different such as widows, spinsters, those suffering from psychological distress and even people simply living alone with a cat, the word 'witch' became a weapon between warring Christian factions too.

The trials continued through a religiously chaotic period of history. Catholicism came under attack for a number reasons, but reformers argued that it promoted a continuation of superstitious heathen beliefs that constituted evidence of heresy, witchcraft and treason. Yet the Catholics, for their abandonment of the one true faith called out the Protestants as witches too. For example, even the Scottish Presbyterian reformer and avid witch hunter John Knox was accused of witchcraft. Knox, aged sixty years had married Lady Margaret Steward, daughter of Lord Ochiltree when she was just fifteen years old. The Catholics, who were being persecuted by Knox, accused him of witchcraft arguing that as Lady Margaret was: 'ane damosel of nobil blud, and he ane auld decrepit creatur of masist bais degrie of onie that could be found in the country', then it stood to reason that the 'decripit' man must have used witchcraft to secure his bride. Knox was also accused of conjuring 'old Nick' who appeared complete with horns and so terrified Knox's secretary that the woman died of fright. The case never made it to trial, however, as Knox escaped formal prosecution due to his powerful allies.

By the end of the English Civil War, witches were apparently being discovered in the wealthy households of the social elite who had fought against the republican reformers and nowhere was this habit of Christian accusing Christian of witchcraft as virulent as in the Kentish villages of Goudhurst and Cranbrook. Historian Peter Elmer has discovered a pattern of witch trials from Goudhurst and Cranbrook that stand apart from all others and indicate these villages to be 'established centres of religious and interdenominational conflict', where accusations of witchcraft were used politically to hurt neighbouring households.

Transcripts demonstrate that Goudhurst was ripe with Baptist reformers whose names feature frequently as accusers, witnesses and magistrates in the trials. The Baptist radical George Weldish (also Wildish and Wildishe) for example, testified against the wife and daughter of local man Stephen Allen and along with his associates Stephen Garrett, Thomas Reid and William Sadler succeeded in having Mary and Elizabeth Allen hanged in 1657.

Elizabeth Allen had been baptised in St Mary's Church Goudhurst on 1 January 1635 and on the parish register her father's name Stephen has been spelled Steaphen. By all accounts, the family was Christian and of a social standing that today might be labelled upper-middle-class. Stephen has been linked to Jeffry Allen, once owner of nearby Twysden Manor.

Sarah French, also from Goudhurst, was accused of bewitching a four-year-old boy who was suffering from a wasting sickness. The French family had lived for generations in a large house with lands that still stands today and is listed by English Heritage.

The puritan witchcraft hysteria of Goudhurst even spread to the New World and became part of the most infamous witch trial ever recorded – Simon Willard of Goudhurst (son of Symon of Goudhurst and grandson of Richard of Horsmonden) travelled to Massachusetts in 1634 with his family. When settled, his own grandson Samuel, a priest and magistrate, was to oversee a number of Salem trials, even being accused himself although the charge was quickly dropped and the accuser denounced. As a convicted witch, his other grandson John, a local constable who spoke against the witch-hunts, was carried through the streets of Salem and hanged on Gallows Hill in 1692.

Chapter 13

The Malleus Maleficarum

'A witch will sit down in a corner of her house with a pail between her legs, stick a knife or some instrument in the wall or a post, and make as if to milk it with her hands. Then she summons her familiar who always works with her in everything, and tells him that she wishes to milk a certain cow from a certain house, which is healthy and abounding in milk. And suddenly the devil takes the milk from the udder of that cow, and brings it to where the witch is sitting, as if it were flowing from the knife.'

Kramer, *Malleus Maleficarum*, 1487

In the village of Caseburg in Northern Germany a woman was accused of stealing her neighbour's milk by way of witchcraft. The farmer described how the woman stabbed a broom handle into the post of her own cowshed and used this handle to milk his cow. This, he reported, was the reason his cow had ceased giving milk for his family.

This type of theft was known in Britain and Scotland as 'milking the tether' and involved creating a pseudo udder, much like the broom handle used by the accused German witch, and nailing it into a post to draw milk from the desired cow using magical intent. The British udder was made from a cow's plaited tail hair and any woman living adjacent to a family whose milk had stopped flowing was in danger of being accused as a witch. Similarly, if a family enjoyed ample milk reserves from their cow then they could be accused of 'drawing the tether'. Either way, milk was the cause of a number of witchcraft accusations.

The famous Scottish witch Isobel Gowdie confessed to plaiting the tether 'the wrong way in the devil's name, and thereby take with us the cow's milk'. It might seem odd that she would confess to dealing with the devil, yet it is important to note that torture was used. In the early trials the clergy used brute force to encourage women to admit their guilt. In the case of Marion Hardie, who in 1629 was confined in the pit of Eyemouth, her treatment was recorded thanks to her son John Trinche who, unusually, made a formal complaint. He described his mother's ordeal:

> 'The compleanor, putt violent hands on her person, band her armes with towes, and so threw the same about that they disjointed and mutilate both her armes, and made the sinews to loupe asunder, and thairafter with their hail force drew and great tow about her waist, kuist her on her backe and with their knees they birsed, bruised, and punsed her so that she wes now able to stirre, strake the heid of ane spear throw her left foote, to the effusioun of her blood in great quantitie and perrel of her lyffe, wherethrow she lay bedfast in great pane and dolour a long tyme thairafter.'

Marion never stood trial as she died from her injuries. Janet Love complained in 1632 that her local minister had suspected her of witchcraft and took it upon himself to:

> 'caused tortour (to) the complainer (Janet) with bow strings, stob her with preins, lay her in the stockes, call wedges on her schinnes, and other ways most miserablie intrete her.'

Milking the tether continued well into the nineteenth century and the folklorist Graham Dayell tells of his encounter in 1834 where on an early Beltaine morning, he saw two witches brushing a tether through the dew. When they realised they were being watched they fled and Dayell picked up the discarded tether and took it home to put above the door of his cowshed. So the story goes, his family had never before enjoyed such quality and quantity of milk.

Making butter was an equally risky business as the folklorist Joseph Train describes. Train interviewed a Lanarkshire family where the wife toiled at the churn all day becoming perplexed that no butter would form. Suspecting something was wrong she called her servant girl and the two reasoned that it must be the fault of the woman who lived next door who, the previous evening, had asked to borrow some eggs. The farmer's wife had refused her and this slight, the two women decided, had attracted the neighbour's wrath. The two women therefore decided to take some eggs to the old woman and apologise for their lack of generosity. Within minutes of returning from their visit, the butter began to form.

The idea that milk and butter can be influenced by witchcraft seems preposterous to us today, yet for those living in the Middle Ages, it was a very serious concern. Heinrich Kramer, writer of the *Malleus Maleficarum* states that:

'One cannot find even a tiny hamlet where the women are not constantly engaged in damaging each other's cows by drying up their milk and, very often, killing them.'

Furthermore, Kramer explains that when it comes to sheep, witches often bring about their sudden death in order to see the wealthy become paupers overnight.

At the height of the witch hunts, neighbours would turn on neighbours, friends on friends and family members on loved ones. Suspicion of witchcraft seemed to underlie almost any misfortune during a time when supernatural causes were suspected for almost every ill. *Malleus Mallificarum* stands as the most significant document fuelling this air of social suspicion and paranoia.

Although trials for witches were already underway by the time he wrote the *Malleus*, his *Hammer of the Witches*, Kramer's document marks a turning point in the European witch-hunts that enabled systematised, organised interrogation against certain accepted measures of guilt. The book was a best seller and the picture it portrayed of witches and women was so fear-inducing, that hysteria spread throughout the western world. Whether one reads the original Latin version, Montague Summers' translation or the Maxwell-Stuart rendition, the content remains breathtaking for the modern reader as Kramer's view of women unfolds:

'What else is woman but a foe to friendship, an inescapable punishment, a necessary evil, a natural temptation, a desirable calamity, a domestic danger, a delectable detriment, an evil of nature, painted with fair colours!'

It was first published in Speyer in 1487 and it sets out a legal and theological basis for the torture and extermination of witches. Yet it is the context of its creation that offers some insight into the reason for its publication. Kramer was a prideful extremist and the *Hammer of the Witches* was his weapon.

It all began in a tiny Austrian village called Tyrol on 9 August 1485. Under the papal bull *Summis Desiderantes Affectibus,* Kramer had been granted the authority to investigate accusations of witchcraft, and he arrived in Tyrol during July to investigate and interrogate fifty suspects, forty-eight of which were women. Tyrol lay in the area of Innsbruck under the auspices of the Archduke Sigismund of Austria with Bishop Georg Golser as its spiritual head.

Bishop Golser and Kramer held different positions regarding the reality of witchcraft. Where Golser believed, as had been the tradition from Prüm, that witchcraft was 'the illusions of evil spirits', Kramer saw it as a real phenomenon requiring a sober and strong response.

As the trials got underway, Golser became increasingly uncomfortable with Kramer's line of questioning and the methods he employed to extract information from the accused. In particular, Kramer became obsessed with sexual behaviours. One woman named Helena Scheuberin was specifically and extensively interrogated in regard to her sexual proclivities until Golser, finding Kramer's interest in this area distasteful and outside the normal remit of such trials, wrote to the Archduke seeking intercedence and stating that trials involving torture should be conducted only on those who had been accused of causing direct bodily harm to others or those involved in blasphemy. The Archduke suggested Golser appoint the priest Sigmund Saumer to oversee Kramer's activities.

Unperturbed, Kramer continued his unusual focus of interrogation. Yet even the panel of commissioners acting as judges for the trial objected to Kramer's unsavoury and volatile line of questioning. Also, Kramer had been caught in a deception; he had paid a woman to hide in an oven and pretend she had done so through bewitchment. The oven, she was to say, was the devil's lair. This ruse caused fear within the community and the woman, now freed by Kramer, was able to point the finger at the witches responsible. Many were accused and tortured due to the lie.

Eventually the judges called for the trials to be postponed and the proceedings rendered void. They were successful and the women were released. The accusations against them of image magic, love spells and causing impotence to men, were dropped. Witnesses, who claimed they had been bewitched by secreted hair, threads from altar cloths, the bones of unbaptised babies, dead mice and Jewish dung, fell suddenly silent, and Bishop Golser advised Kramer to leave Innsbruck as his safety could not be guaranteed. It was an embarrassing fiasco.

When, in the *Malleus Maleficarum* Kramer makes mention of 'two defenders of heretics and witches who fail to prosecute them with sufficient vigour', it is Bishop Golser and Archduke Sigismund to whom he refers. The work was written quickly and published in less than two years of this event. The first edition of the *Malleus* contained a copy of Kramer's papal bull at the beginning to demonstrate his authority as *Insquisitoris*. The letter of approbation from the University of Cologne accompanying it was, however, a forgery.

Kramer's stance against witches can be seen as the unfortunate culmination of a narrative that had begun to build within the Church in the twelfth century. This was the time when theologians became particularly preoccupied with eschatological concerns. The Cistercian abbot Joachim of Fiore (1135-1202) was pivotal in creating a narrative of fear. He claimed to have received a number of divine visions in which he perceived the revelation of St John in new ways, where patterns in The Old Testament mirrored symbols in the New, the interpretation of which gave him an accurate date of 1260 for the coming of the Antichrist. For Joachim therefore, the 'end was nigh'.

Although apocalyptic thought and a desire to predict the date of the end of the world was nothing new, Joachim saw the events and impulse towards it as inaugurated by humanity rather than being an unfolding of divine will as had previously been the case. Although Joachim was to ultimately turn against the Catholic Church, his ideas took root, especially in the more extreme, radically orientated Franciscans who saw themselves on the front line of Joachim's holy war and regarded him as a prophet.

The consequence of Joachim's paradigm-shift was that the great battle waged in the apocalypse of St John was now the fault of humans such as female herbalists and sectarian Christians who, due to their devilish beliefs, were personally responsible for the coming of Satan.

The change in narrative from divine plan to human wrong-doing is subtle but powerful, as this understanding of the role of human beings in the apocalypse meant that cunning-women were no longer ignorant local women seduced by the devil but instead were an active enemy of the Church, working to bring down the world and damn souls to the fiery pit. To this end, in 1258, Pope Alexander IV instructed the Inquisition to persecute cunning-women along the same lines as heretics. Witches therefore became legally persecuted through direct socio-political action.

Paranoia became an emergent property of Joachim's theory as the Church began to see enemies everywhere, and with the Antichrist's arrival imminent, a response was urgent. In this spirit, an unfolding of sectarian persecution in the twelfth century began in earnest, particularly against gnostic, dualistic Christian sects such as the Albigensians and Waldensians. This was the beginning of dark times for the Church which acted through crusades, torture, persecution and any means possible to save itself, humanity and the world from Satan.

What Kramer saw within the Tyrol witch trials was a continuation of beliefs and behaviours that propelled humanity towards Armageddon. Where two centuries earlier, Joachim believed that women, sinners and heretics had begun the process of damnation, for Kramer it was witches and those protecting them who were hell bent on finishing it.

Kramer therefore built upon Joachim's foundations. Gone was Prüm's theory that witchcraft was an illusion. It was very important for Kramer to identify witchcraft as a real physical phenomenon; otherwise the third part of his *Malleus* that deals with legal proceedings would lose its validity. Witchcraft needed to cause actual bodily harm in order to fulfil the requirements needed for the legislature. The *Malleus* therefore seeks to establish a different view of witchcraft from Prüm; witches and their craft were not fabrications fuelled by demonic visions residing in the mental infirmity of common minds. Instead, witches were real women practicing authentic diabolic magic with the sole intention of causing physical and psychological harm to good Christian folk.

In the *Malleus* he says, 'The question arises whether people who hold that witches do not exist are to be regarded as notorious heretics.' His answer is a resounding yes. Indeed, on the title page of its first publication were the words, *'Haersis est maxima opera maleficarum non credere'* (To disbelieve in witchcraft is the greatest of heresies).

It cannot be underestimated how potent this alteration of belief was. Where previously the stories of witches flying the skies and transporting themselves to distant locations were regarded as illusory fictions, now they had to be accepted as real threats. Witches were vile creatures and Kramer even warns priests of possible retorts under 'questioning' such as 'Sweep your tongue round in my arse'.

Kramer evidences the empirical nature of his argument with an account from Waldshut on the Rhine; a local woman who was hated by the villagers was refused invitation to a wedding. In revenge, she conjured a demon to transport her to the top of a mountain where she could work a spell to produce a hailstorm and ruin the celebrations. At her trial, shepherds testified that they saw the woman flying to the mountaintop where she urinated in a hole and with a demon's aid, raised the liquid into a terrible storm. The woman confessed to these acts, and many more besides, before being burned at the stake.

Kramer states often that those who follow the spirit of Prüm's Canon *Episcopi* and believe that such things 'happened only in the imagination and fantasy', are dangerous and have the consequence of wrongly believing that witches 'were blameless' and 'consequently, on many occasions they remain unpunished'. For Kramer, if magic could cause actual physical harm then it was reasonable for the women to be tried in court as with any other form of harm such as property damage, assault, and murder.

The stakes were now high, as to deal with a real and present danger; legislature could be legitimately passed to respond to the peril. Eyewitness accounts and confessions from the accused themselves, such as occurred at Waldshut on the Rhine, added the empirical validity Kramer required. The *Malleus* therefore, laid the legal, empirical and psychological foundations for the Witchcraft Act of 1542 as well as the publication of King James's *Daemonologie* of 1597, both of which mixed witchcraft with notions of apocalyptic fervour:

> 'Of even greater significance was the apocalyptic message ... that folk were living in the Last Days, and that the world as they knew it was coming to an end. The cosmic struggle between God and the Devil was growing ever more intense and signs of the encroaching doomsday, as predicted by the book of Revelation, were detectable on a daily basis, not least the threat of witchcraft. It is a theme, which lies at the heart of [King James'] Daemonologie; witches and demonic interference spring from two sources, human sin and the impending end of the world.
>
> (Lizanne Henderson, Detestable Slaves of the Devil, 2011)

Throughout the *Malleus* it is women that are predominantly identified as witches and in the first section, Kramer explains why it is that women are so prone to this type of behaviour. He asks:

> 'why are there more workers of harmful magic found in the female sex, which is so frail and unstable, than among men? It certainly solves no problem to offer opinions to the contrary, since actual experience (quite apart from the verbal testimonies of trustworthy people) renders such things credible.'

Kramer's answer builds upon the Augustinian theory that women are prone to being the devil's playthings due to their nature, as Kramer later puts it, their 'fleshly lusts' and 'carnal filthiness'. Augustine had already established that women were genetically responsible for birthing evil and consequently exhibited a mutable nature, easily corrupted by temptation. Kramer simply brought this theory alive, developing it and showing how evil emerges from the female's defective creation from Adam's curved rib making them an 'unfinished animal ... always being deceptive' and further, when women 'think alone they think evil'. Evil is therefore woman's 'natural inclination'. In his conclusion to the reasons why women are witches rather than men, he resolves that women conjure and work with evil spirits 'to assuage their sexual appetite'.

He goes on to describe how women are so obsessed with sex that they encourage demonic lovers to sate them. Incubi and succubae are mythic evil spirits thought to visit people at night and copulate with them. Kramer explains that:

> 'Women subject themselves willingly to incubi, as happens in the case of witches. One finds, however, that men do not willingly subject themselves to succubi because the strength of reasoning they have by nature, and in which men are superior to women, make them detest this kind of thing the more.'

The second part of the *Malleus* deals with the investigatory aspects of witchcraft, what to expect, how to understand it and basically, what witches actually do. Kramer often uses a scholastic method to make certain points in the *Malleus* – he puts forward an actual account of sorcery and uses this as a case study to then clarify the involvement of witchcraft. For example, he recounts a tale of sorcery that occurred in a town that 'decency demands one keeps secret'. What his reasons for secrecy were we shall never know, but the event he described concerned a poor woodsman: One day whilst chopping wood, three ferocious cats attacked the man. They clawed and bit him and he only managed to save himself from further harm by beating them harshly. The event traumatised him, although he did manage to continue his wood chopping for a further hour.

Later that day he was arrested for beating 'three highly respectable women' of the town who had been so badly injured that they were 'lying in their beds, unable to get up or move'. The man was mortified, wailing loudly and proclaiming that he would never hurt or strike any woman. The magistrate was furious with his lies and the hearing continued until the woodsman said, 'I remember I did strike some creatures at the time, but they were not women.'

Here, Kramer is concerned with the question of whether evil spirits had assumed the shape of cats at the witches' behest, or whether the witches themselves had assumed the form of cats. Kramer contends that it was spirits that transported the witches to the woodsman and helped them shapeshift into feline form and he warns that when such 'crimes remain unpunished ... God is the more offended'. So great is the offense that those who fail to believe in the reality of such transportations are guilty of heresy. Kramer explains how witches achieve physical transportation:

'There are various ways in which I can show that [witches] can be transported physically...Under instruction from an evil spirit, they make an ointment from the body-parts of children, particularly those they have killed before they have been baptized. They smear it in a chair or piece of wood, and when they have done this, they are carried at once into the air, day or night, in full sight of everyone, or invisibly.'

Another case study concerns a similarly 'poor man' who has been plagued by sexual magic and cannot stop having sex. 'Over and over again, with renewed vigour, he performs every sexual act.' The man, we are told, cannot stop fornicating and he accuses a woman who slighted him as being the cause of the curse. This case recalls the 1661 witch trial of Helen Gray who was accused of casting a spell on a local man that caused 'his wand lay never doun'. The constant erection, so it was reported, almost killed him.

Further examples of witches' deeds are then put forward and include among others the problem of men whose penises have been removed by witches. Here, unusually, Kramer reverts to illusion as the cause, and the remedy is to break the spell and see that the penis is intact. Another concern is how witches cause men to experience either excessive love or hatred and also, how women can cause erectile dysfunction in men.

Kramer viewed the problem of evil through the prism of his own obsession and prejudices, which used women as repositories for fear. Any harm that befell a person was now potentially attributed to the woman next door, or the old widow shunned at the edge of the village. Cats were suspect and women, if raped, were secretly enjoying it due to their ferocious, wild carnal appetite. Gone were the days of Mildþryþ and the Anglo-Saxons, where women enjoyed some protection from rape and domestic violence.

Chapter 14

Bessie's Tale
(Cunning-Women on Trial)

'let her take equal parts of cloves, ginger, aniseed, and liquorice, and mix them together in ale; seethe them together; strain the mixture; put it in a vessel, then take a little quantity of it in a mutchkin can, with some white sugar cast among it; take and drink thereof each day in the morning; walk a while after, before meat, and she would soon be better.'

The spirit of Tom Reid, Pitcairn Trials, vol 1, 1833.

In the tiny Scottish hamlet of Lyne, a cunning-woman named Bessie Jack (commonly called Bessie Dunlop) was tending to the needs of her community, just as Mildþryþ had been doing years earlier. Times were harsh, and the people eked out a precarious existence in a land scattered at the time with peat bogs. Agriculture clung to foothills where crops faltered in shallow soil.

Bessie lived almost one hundred years following the publication of the *Malleus*, during a time of tense spiritual and religious conflict. The Reformation was in full swing and as a Catholic woman, probably ignorant of the blended nature of her beliefs, Bessie must have found the Protestant reforms of 1560 frustrating. Yet life went on, and as historian Emma Wilby describes, Bessie:

'worked at the rock face of sixteenth century Scottish life: she delivered babies, healed the sick, consoled the bereaved, identified criminals and recovered lost and stolen goods.'

Regardless of new religious fashion, people still needed healthcare, the bereaved still required comfort and those who stared death and starvation in the eyes required all the help Bessie could give. The locals called her the 'goodwife' and many sought her out in times of need.

Bessie's career began unusually. She was married to Andrew Jack, a miller and farmworker and they enjoyed a reasonably good life in Lynn Glen, Ayrshire until the year of 1547 when Andrew fell seriously ill. The timing could not have been worse – Bessie had recently given birth and was still suffering the physical pains of a particularly tough delivery, also, the baby was sickly. When their best cow then died too, Bessie was in despair and one day, whilst driving their remaining cattle to Monkcastle, Bessie sat on a boulder and wept. It was in this moment of emotional and one might speculate, psychological vulnerability, that Bessie had her first supernatural experience; a ghost appeared to her.

The spirit introduced himself as that of the late Tom Reid who had died during the 1547 battle of Pinkie whilst in the employ of the Blair clan. During her trial, Bessie described Tom as an elderly man, well dressed, honest, respectable with a long grey beard and a white staff who'd greeted her with the words, 'Gude day, Bessie … Why must tho make such dole and weeping for any earthly thing?'

Tom and Bessie had a number of encounters during which Tom explained that the Queen of the Elves had sent him to her from the fairy court of Elfhame. Apparently, Bessie had met the Queen earlier that year when her son had opened the door to a stout woman who'd requested some water to drink. Bessie had obliged her and in return the woman had offered a prophecy, 'Bessie, your bairn will die, but your husband will mend of his sickness.'

Tom introduced her to twelve elves who said, 'Welcome Bessie, will you go with us?' Bessie did not answer them and when she asked Tom who they were he said, 'They are the good neighbours that dwell in the court of Elfhame, and they desire you to go with them.' Bessie was dubious and replied, 'I see no reason to go with them unless I know why.' Tom explained that in the court of Elfhame she would enjoy 'plenty of meat and clothes' just as he did. Ultimately Bessie refused the Queen's invitation as she did not wish to leave her husband, and instead accepted Tom Reid's tuition and guidance in their ways of herbalism, prophecy and magic.

Bessie became well known as a gifted healer. She cured the children of John Jack and Wilson of Townhead with herbs given to her by Tom. Local women sought her to birth their children and Tom gave Bessie green silks and threads to tie around the expectant mother's left arm. As Bessie's reputation spread, the gentry and nobility also requested her remedies, and for a common local housewife, this could well have been welcomed as quite a success. Bessie and her husband might have enjoyed the blossoming of her career, the extra income and high reputation it brought.

Lady Kilbowie for example, had suffered from a crocked leg for much of her life. One might imagine such a woman had seen the best physicians money could buy, yet hearing of Bessie's gifts, she called upon her to help. Bessie asked Tom about the Lady's crooked leg and Tom advised Bessie that unfortunately 'the marrow of the limb was perished and the blood benumbed' so the old woman would never recover.

The prognosis for the daughter of Lord Stanley was rather better. The young girl was wasting away when her mother sent a servant to fetch Bessie. With the help of Tom, Bessie diagnosed that this was 'due to cauld blood that went about her heart, that caused her to pine away'. Bessie brewed the herbal remedy detailed at the beginning of this chapter that included as its active ingredients 'equal parts of cloves, ginger, aniseed, and liquorice, and mix them together in ale'. Cloves are anti-inflammatory, anaesthetic and warming. Ginger is good for digestion as is liquorice and aniseed. All are therefore beneficial for digestion and may have invigorated the girl's appetite. The Lord's daughter recovered and in payment for the cure, Bessie received some cheese and a 'peck of meal'.

Soon, Bessie's supernatural gifts became sought after for more than just healing. William Blair (of the family who had once employed Tom Reid) sought her advice to discover whether his eldest daughter's suitor, the Lord Crawford (Craufurd) of Baidland, was a suitable match. When Bessie predicted that the marriage would be the cause of the girl's suicide, the engagement was called off. His youngest daughter married the Lord instead. The method of divination Bessie used is unrecorded. She may have simply asked Tom, but perhaps she did as historian Joseph Wright suggested in 1898 was the local custom in the area in matters of marriage – she might have used the sieve and shears:

> 'This among the other superstitious customs common on Halloween, is also used as a mode of divination in regard to marriage. When two persons are evened or named in relation to the connubial tie, if the riddle turns round, it is concluded that they are to be united in this bond.'

Similarly to Mildþryþ, Bessie was often called upon to locate lost property – when some gold coins were stolen from Lady Thirdpart of the barony of Renfrewshire, Bessie was asked to find the thief and when some plough-irons went missing from James Jamieson and James Baird of

Watterton, Bessie was called upon to find them; two blacksmiths, Gabriel and George Black, stood accused of secreting the irons in their father's Locharside house and Bessie was to locate the exact spot. It was a significant case, which included the intercedence of the Archbishop of Glasgow when the local sheriff was discovered to have taken a bribe to aid the thieves.

Although it is generally assumed that Bessie 'was arrested due to her longstanding reputation as a healer' (*The Scotsman*, September, 2015), it remains unclear just how Bessie came to the attention of the judiciary and became accused of witchcraft. It has been suggested that her problems began when a burgess named William Kyle asked for Bessie's help concerning a cloak stolen from Hugh Scott. Unfortunately, however, when Bessie named the thief as Molly Boyd, Kyle was unable to recover the item as the woman had already made the cloak into a skirt.

Oddly, Bessie had only agreed to assist Kyle if he kept her involvement anonymous. The reason for this request will never be known, but it might be that Bessie's increasing help with cases of theft was attracting too much negative attention. In this instance, her concern was justified as Kyle, angered by the failure to retrieve the cloak, had Bessie arrested. She was freed by the influential involvement of the Blair clan. It would seem that Bessie had useful patrons, but sadly, some persistent enemies also.

In 1576 she was arrested a second time and accused by persons unknown of:

'the using of sorcerie, witchcraft and incantatione, with invocation of spretis of the devill, continewand in familiarite with thame, at all sic tymes as sche thocht expedient, deling with charmes, and abusing pepill with devillisch craft of sorcerie foirsaid .. usit thie divers yeiris bypast'.

The court employed a professional torturer, a 'witch doctor, a skeillie man, was fetched frae yont Glesco' to deal wi' the case'. The witch doctor was to provide the bodily evidence of witchcraft such as the 'devil's mark'. Within the *Malleus* it is stated that a witch will have a 'devil's mark' on her body, and so the woman should be shaved and searched, the logic being that such a mark (such as a simple mole) was evidence of guilt. Bessie was indeed stripped and searched as well as being 'scored abune the breath', which refers to having a cross scored into the forehead by a knife.

The focus of Bessie's trial appears to have been the presence of the spirit of Tom Reid. The judges wanted to know how she knew the herbs and rituals needed to heal the Laird of Stanley's daughter for example, and during her interrogations, of which there were several over many weeks, Bessie told her tale; her knowledge, whereby she was able to 'tell diverse persons of things they tynt [lost] or were stolen away, or help sick persons' did not come from her, it came from old Tom Reid and as historian Lizanne Henderson explains:

> 'While the practice of folk medicine was never condoned by the authorities, some level of toleration may have extended to healers for the simple reason they performed a much needed and highly necessary service in communities devoid of alternative medical assistance. However, if the source of a healer's powers was thought to be dubious, such as through the conjuration of spirits, or deemed to be demonically inspired, such as by the fairies, the consequences could prove fatal.'

Whether Bessie ever considered she would one day stand accused of the 'devillisch craft of sorcerie' we shall never know. Her trial was one of the earliest and she might have assumed that the witch trials were designed to catch those practicing the dark arts, something she might well have applauded. Yet she was found guilty and sentenced on 8 November 1576 and was duly strangled and then burnt at the stake on Edinburgh's Castle Hill.

Bessie's treatment has struck many as particularly brutal considering she did no harm. Yet the measures of guilt within the growing hysteria were becoming fluid as issues of personal slight and morality blended with a general escalation in fear regarding the now stereotyped idea of the evil witch. Historian Michael Bailey states that the sixteenth century is 'most well known not for new systems of magic, but for new levels of legal condemnation and prosecution of magical crimes'.

Bessie's ordeal became the norm as later trials followed along similar lines. For example, on 2 March 1618, Joan Willimott of Goodby village in Leicestershire confessed 'that she hath a spirit which she calleth Pretty' and that this spirit was given to her by her 'master' named William Berry who blew a fairy into her mouth. The fairy changed into the spirit of a woman who then materialised before Joan and asked for her obedience. It was reported during her trial that:

> 'She never hurt anybody… but did help divers persons that were stricken or fore-spoken (bewitched); and that her spirit came weekly to her, and would tell of divers persons that were stricken and fore-spoken. And she saith that the use which she had of the Spirit, was to know those did which she had undertaken to amend

and she did help them by certain prayers which she used ... neither did she employ her spirit in anything, but only to bring word how those did which she had undertaken to cure'.

Joan used her spirit guide to divine healing cures and help those who had been bewitched by sorcery. Unfortunately for Joan, a number of women came forward claiming that she had bewitched them. Ellen Green testified that she had witnessed Joan call upon two spirits that appeared in the form of a kitten and a mole. Ellen was able to bring a surprising amount of detail to her account, even stating that these two spirit animals were named Pusse and Hisse and that both suckled from Joan's body. Emma described how, on one occasion Joan had sought revenge on a local baker who'd once accused her of witchcraft – she'd allowed the animals to suckle from her before sending them to the baker to 'bewitch hime to death'. By the conclusion of the testimony, old Joan had apparently accumulated quite a body count.

Four years previously, spirits also instructed a woman named Jonet Boyman. Jonet was described in her trial as 'ane wyss woman that culd mend diverss seikness and bairnis that are tane away with the faryie men and wemin'. Jonet is described here as a *wyss woman* (wise-woman) a name interchangeable with cunning-woman. She can heal diverse sickness and oddly, babies that have been taken away by the fairies – a phrase that alludes to the folklore of changelings. Changelings were thought to be fairy infants, exchanged by the fairy-folk for human babies. The myth, which exists in Northern Europe, likely arose as an explanation for abnormalities, disabilities and illnesses afflicting children.

Jonet was executed on 29 December 1572, to the probable dismay of her husband William Steill. Despite her healing work the court found her guilty of witchcraft, as it concluded that her role as a physician was 'under cullor and pretence of medicine'.

Another Jonet, Jonet Carswell, also found herself in dire circumstances due to her healing practices. Known for her cures using potions made from snails, clay and thread, she was tried and killed in 1579.

These healers were singled out for harsh punishment because their abilities involved some form of spirit communication. Their spirits could sometimes take the form of animals (also termed familiars), like Pusse and Hisse yet often they appeared as fairies, elves or those mediating with the little folk.

Fairies have a long heritage. First mentioned in Homer's *Iliad* they are described as elemental nature spirits – 'watery fairies dance in mazy rings'. The twelfth century English clergyman Gervase of Tilbury wrote in his

Otia Imperialia regarding the existence of English fairies, even suggesting that the serpent in Genesis may have had a woman's face like English werewolves do.

In the Christian lexicon, fairies became demons and so when Bessie and Jonet spoke of fairies, the judiciary was hearing 'demons'. This made the healing practices of the women secondary. It did not matter if they were benevolent, harmless healers; they were, in the eyes of the Church and State, cavorting with Satan's minions nonetheless. As Augustine had been at pains to explain to his fellow clergy, the cunning-women in Biblical stories may have been doing good, but it was the source of that good work that was blasphemous. Bessie had been relating with demons, not God.

Female physicians who did not use spirits in their work also attracted the attention of the witch-hunters. As we know all too painfully, sometimes the work of physicians fails to bring the outcome we desire and loved-ones die. Occasionally, either rightly or wrongly, emotional people seeking answers can blame the doctors whose responsibility it had been to cure their relative. Today when things go wrong, there are systems in place to investigate any negligence or wrong-doing. Yet a few hundred years ago, a cunning-woman could simply be accused of witchery, and this is what happened to Ursula Kempe.

In 1582 Ursula (also known as Ursula Gray) from Essex, was in trouble. She had fallen into what had become an almost predictable trap that saw a number of local healers tortured and charged as witches. Three of her remedies had failed to heal her patients and the families involved, angry and grieving, accused her of killing their loved ones using witchcraft. Further accusations then compounded Ursula's problems. Another patient came forward claiming Ursula had used sorcery to break her baby's neck. The baby, named Joan, had been ill and Ursula had cured her for a fee of 12 pence yet Mrs Thurlow, Joan's mother, had argued with Ursula over the fee. Some time later, baby Joan fell from her crib and broke her neck. Mrs Thurlow claimed it was Ursula's revenge for the argument.

Anne Jespersdatter, a Danish cunning-woman was also accused of witchcraft following the death of a patient. A blacksmith's wife who testified to witnessing a number of Anne's healing rituals brought her to the attention of the prosecutors. The healing in question concerned her husband's colleague Svend Smed, another blacksmith who was very ill and had asked for Anne's help. During the healing ritual Anne had made Svend lay 'in the ground' in the couple's scullery as a symbolic burial. A number of Scandinavian trials contain evidence of this type of healing ritual where the patient is symbolically buried in order to rise again renewed. It was commonly referred to as the 'in the ground' ritual. Unfortunately for Anne, Svend died.

An 'in the ground ritual' was also used in an attempt to cure Niels Munk's two eldest children, Peder and Hi, of a witch's curse. Niels was a nobleman of Rosborg, Denmark. He had experienced a particularly difficult time; his wife, Sidsel Skinkel, had already become ill and all his cattle had died. When his children also fell sick with an unidentifiable disease in 1639, witchcraft appeared as the only explanation.

Niels approached the Bishop, Hans Wandal, with his suspicions since the children had shouted the name 'Fusøre' when asked who had bewitched them. Previously, Niels had upset the local farmer Anders Christensen of Fusøre by taking his farm, and Niels recalled that Anders had stated at the time an intention to see him leave Rosborg within three years.

The Bishop saw no evidence of sorcery and so Niels sought the help of three local physicians who performed an 'in the ground ritual' to cure his children. When the healing failed, Niels turned on them and havoc ensued. The three, Søren Frebjerg, Birgitte Mouridsdatter and Mette Mouridsdatter admitted that they had attended a witches meeting with Anders Christensen of Fusøre, his wife Mette Pedersdatter and daughters Karen and Maren. Attending also were Kirsten Andersdatter, Anne Andersdatter, Mette Andersdatter and Anne Mouridsdatter. The transcripts describe how the party of witches had flown to Rosborg, danced and then turned into ducks to summon the devil against Niels Munk.

All lived on farms owned by Niels. The original three were sentenced to death. Anne Mouridsdatter committed suicide in prison and the others were detained, their ultimate fate unrecorded.

On 6 August 2009 Nicholas Taylor reported to the *Guardian* newspaper that he had been buried alive in the Dorset countryside. Luckily, he was not victim of an accusation of witchcraft but was instead experiencing a ritualistic death as part of his training to become a shamanic healer. After digging his own grave, Nicholas spent a night covered by planks with earth above and only a small hole for air. When he emerged the next morning, he felt:

> 'the ordinary miracle of day and I felt rinsed through; clean as water. Everywhere I looked life was phenomenal, an exceptional gift that I was fortunate enough to bear witness to.'

He speaks of this experience as pivotal to his process of learning, but also as a method of personal healing following intense psychological and emotional trauma.

Mildþryþ used similar life and death symbolism within some of her remedies:

> 'Se wifmann we hire cild afedan ne mæg, gange to gewitenes mannes birgenne ond stæppe þonne þriwa ofer þa byrgenne ond cweðe þonne þriwa þas word: "þis me to bote þære laþan lætbyrde, þis me to bote þære swæran swærtbyrde, þis me to bote þære laðan lambyrde" ond þonne þæt wif seo mid berane ond heo to hyre hlaforde on reste ga, þonne cweþe heo: "up ic gonge, ofer þe stæppe mid cwican cilde, nalæs mid cwellendum, mid fulborenum, nalæs mis fægan.'

> *'Let the woman who cannot nourish her child go to the grave of a dead man and then step three times over the grave and say these words three times: "This is my remedy for hateful slow birth, this is my remedy for a difficult birth, this is my remedy for imperfect birth." And when the woman will be with child and goes to bed, to her husband, then she is to say: "Up I go, step over you, with a living child not a dying [one], with a full-born [one] not with a doomed [one]."*

The dead man's grave is symbolic of the boundary between life and death. Before conception, the woman desiring a healthy baby steps three times across death. Following conception, she then steps across a living man, her husband, asserting her choice to bring a living, healthy child into the world.

In his contemporary ordeal, Nicholas described that the process of being buried seemed to involve a choice for him also. He said it was a choice between living a life through love or through fear.

The last execution for witchcraft in the British Isles took place in 1727 when Janet Horne was stripped, tarred and paraded through the streets of Dornoch before being burned alive. The evidence of witchcraft put forward at her trial, was that she had given birth to a deformed child. The reason for the decline of the witch trials (in Scotland the witchcraft acts were repealed just nine years following Janet Horne's burning) remains a matter of debate. It seems probable, however, that rationalism began to revive to the point where the lowering of evidentiary standards that was occurring, simply had to end. A new scepticism was born in Massachusetts in the years following the extreme hysteria of the Salem trials and American scholars began to argue that witchcraft was an imaginary crime, and imagination was not grounds for accusation. Yet it would be some decades before the epidemic abated in Europe.

Isobel (Bell) McGhie from Beith in North Ayrshire was accused of witchcraft as late as 1836. Isobel's accusation was recent enough for her to have been interviewed by a third party at the time, an archaeologist (although other records suggest he might have been a mason) named James Dobie.

Dobie reported Bell's words: 'I don't pretend to skill. All I do is in the fear of God, and if He blesses the means the praise is His.' During her trial, Bell mentioned how she first encountered healing charms when as a child, her mother once procured one for her. From this early experience, Bell was inspired to the healing arts and similarly to Bessie, became highly sought after by the wealthy elite who found she could heal humans, animals and even turn soured milk wholesome again.

It is clear from Bell's testimony that she did not see herself as anything other than a good Christian woman working to help and heal others. When speaking of evil, she mentions an early encounter with a sorcerer named Douglas who scared her. It seems that Bell saw a clear distinction between her own benevolent work as a healer and that of black magicians like Douglas, and one might imagine her surprise at being viewed in similar terms to him.

Chapter 15

A Very British Tradition

'Witchcraft may be Britain's native spiritual heritage.'
Emma Wilby, 2005

Shamanism is the word used today to describe ancient indigenous spiritual practices. The shaman is a mysterious figure who uses herbs, ritual and magic to heal and prophesy. The cunning-women also used herbs and ritual for similar ends and Emma Wilby believes that witchcraft is therefore Britain's native shamanic, spiritual heritage. She theorises that witch trial transcripts indicate how 'shamanic visionary traditions, of pre-Christian origin, survived in many parts of Britain during the early modern period'.

Witchcraft is being seen today with new eyes. Historian Julian Goodare for example, is re-categorising witchcraft in an attempt to reawaken the nuances lost to us in the hysteria of the Middle Ages. The Anglo-Saxons had numerous words to describe their spiritual healers and magic workers and to truly identify an ancient tradition, Goodare has teased out some distinctions from our more unitary category of 'witch'. Pertinent for Mildþryþ and those healers caught up in the witch trials, Goodare has identified the 'envisioned witch' as one who exhibits positive elements of community care, healing and spiritual wisdom. Envisioned witches are therefore the ones throughout history that Dickinson has described as having 'special powers' of visionary and magical gifts. Mildþryþ and cunning-women would fit well into this category and could thereby leave behind the warts and suckling demons of Kramer's world for good.

Witchcraft as Britain's spiritual heritage is not a new idea. Others have walked the same path, although without access to modern evidence, most have floundered. Historian and Egyptologist Margaret Murray (1863-1963) believed that witchcraft and its modern revival of Wicca emerged from an unbroken tradition of British spirituality that stretched into antiquity.

A woman ahead of her time, Murray was a scholar, archaeologist, anthropologist and the first female lecturer in Archaeology in England at UCL. She was also a first wave feminist, deeply concerned with improving women's rights, particularly within education. Her books *The Witch Cult in Western Europe* and *The God of the Witches* form the first scholarly attempt to tease truth from the witch trials.

Murray used an ethnographic methodology to uncover themes within trial transcripts that did not emerge from the projections or leading questions used by the judiciary. Certain commonalities in the stories told by accused witches were evidence, so Murray believed, of an ancient folkloric tradition. Tales of pacts with the devil being made in return for magical powers were particularly frequent. Also, marks made by the devil upon the witch's body and the orgiastic Sabbats that followed all pointed in Murray's mind towards a consistent narrative of truth.

Consistency, however, is not a fool-proof measure of truth and she received much criticism. Her hypothesis was certainly controversial and in the preface to her 1933 edition of *The Witch Cult in Western Europe* she felt compelled to state:

'I have received many letters containing criticisms, some complimentary, some condemnatory, of that book [the *Witch Cult in Western Europe*]. If other correspondents honour me with similar private criticisms of the present volume, I ask of them that they will sign their communications, even when the opinions they express are adverse. Anonymous letters, of which I received a number, reflect no credit on their writers.'

A second figure to attract criticism for pursuing the same hypothesis was a Lancashire man named Gerald Gardner. He is known as the father of modern witchcraft as he developed the religion of Wicca from what he always maintained was an ancient British tradition. Few took him seriously and his story of initiation into a New Forest coven with footsteps stretching back centuries has been largely dismissed as wishful thinking. The New Forest sits to the south of ancient Hwicce territory and whether Gardner was telling the truth or not, Wicca is the fastest growing religion in the United States and embodies within its very existence a defiant spirit within the British that never gave up on the old ways.

Gardner made the first important step towards taking back the term 'witch' and associating it once more with the principles of healing, magic and spirituality. He did not have recourse to Mildþryþ's Old English herbals or archaeological evidence from the Hwicce, yet he delivered a religious system which draws upon ancient motifs and beliefs and brings them into the modern world.

Wicca may not be everybody's cup of tea, but that doesn't seem to matter too much. The movement is morphic; some Wiccans intuit a single deity conceived in male and female forms whilst others prefer a more polytheistic interpretation that draws in mythic frameworks from the Mediterranean to enrich their experience of worship. Some employ no deific attributions at all and adhere to an energetic cosmology that approaches concepts of quantum physics. Wicca is a pliable, evolving tradition that moves with the understanding of individuals and views magic as the creative life force which imbues the universe.

Academics formally rejected Murray's work, finding her extrapolations that covens of witches lurked in the royal courts and ate babies while conversing with the world of fairies too fanciful to be taken seriously. They certainly had a point, yet her basic intuition that the materials from witch trial testimonies contained remnants of actual ancient beliefs, is now being verified. Historian Emma Wilby has discovered for example, that certain thematic markers within trial testimonies do indeed reveal what Murray had hoped to prove.

At first, Wilby's evidence can seem just as fanciful as Murray's. Fairies, elves and ecstatic visions hardly appear more substantive themes of a continuing legacy of shamanic beliefs. But when compared to the pre-Christian material from Mildþryþ's books and the agendas displayed within the documents condemning pre-Christian principles, Wilby's fairies become compelling as she argues that they demonstrate an ancient folkloric element to the trial accounts that has gone unnoticed.

Fairies, elves and spirits occur frequently within trial transcripts. Wilby contends that the judiciary, who were only interested in proving guilt through demonic collaboration, were not in the slightest bit interested in hearing about fairies and elves and had no reason to include them in transcripts as they did not fit the picture of witches they desired to portray. Consequently, it follows that the appearance of fairies in the witch trials did not come from leading questions or enforced confessions. Fairies, it seems, came from the women themselves and so is evidence of a genuine tradition. As Robin Briggs describes in his book *Witches and Neighbours*, the European witch-hunts were 'a coalescence between longstanding popular beliefs and the agencies for enforcing social and religious conformity.'

Wilby suggests that what Bessie Dunlop was describing in her account of Tom Reid was a powerful 'visionary experience' and 'was an expression of a vigorous popular visionary tradition rooted in pre-Christian shamanistic beliefs and practices'. Tom Reid spoke often to Bessie of the fairies and wanted Bessie to accompany him to their kingdom of Elfhame (Elf home) in the realm of Middle Earth. Bessie relayed Tom's words during her trial stating that the fairies were the 'gude wichtis that wer rydand in Middil-zerd'. Another accused witch, Alison Peirson, said that her uncle had been taken by the fairies to a place called middil-eird.

The inhabitants of Middle Earth are referred to in many trials. Isobel Haldane, tried in Perth, 1623, said the devil (which might have been a scribe's ad lib alteration of fairy) had taken her to a hill where she had entered faery land. Jonet Drever was burnt for 'fosetering of ane bairne in the hill of Westray to the fary fol, callit of hir our guid nichbouris'. Barbara Parish also spoke of meetings with the 'good neighbours', a term referring to communities of fairies and elves.

Pitcairn relays the infamous, high profile trial of Katherine Ross, Lady Munro of Fowlis who admitted that she 'wald gang in Hillis to speik the elf folk'. Married to the fifteenth Baron of Fowlis who was the chief of the Scottish clan of Munro, she was accused of plotting to murder her stepson Robert with witchcraft, her motive being that following his death she could marry his widow to her brother George Ross. As George was not yet a widower it was inferred that Lady Munro conspired to kill George's wife also. To this end she employed two other witches who made a clay doll (a poppet or voodoo doll) towards which elven arrows were to be shot as a curse. A poison was also made. The two witches were burnt in 1577. Lady Fowlis was not tried until July 1590 being 'dilatit of certain crymes of witchcraft'. She was acquitted.

In the early fifteenth century, a cunning-woman named Agnes Hancock claimed that whenever she felt in need of advice or information she consulted the fairies that lived in a hill. Agnes also specialised in the diagnosing and curing of sickness caused by malevolent fairies. Bessie claimed similarly that her ghost Tom Reid liaised between her and the fairies and so she was able to successfully treat patients who had been specifically injured by 'elf-grippit'. Elf-grippet means to be taken by an elf.

The belief in elves and fairies interceding for good (and sometimes) bad within the lives of humanity persisted through the burning times. In 1579, *The Shepherds Calendar* stated that 'The opinion of faeries and elfes is very old', and a clergyman named John Penry living in sixteenth century Wales said that the local people held fairies in 'astonishing reverence'. In his 1677 work *The Displaying of Supposed Witchcraft*, John Webster wrote that in some parts of England the belief that fairies and elves caused illness was so strong that a doctor was of no use in such cases:

> 'the common people, if they chance to have any sort of the Epilepsie, Palsie, Convulsions or the like, do presently perswade themselves that they are bewitched, forespoken, blasted, fairy taken, or haunted with some evil spirit...and if you should by plain reason shew them, that they are deceived, and that there is no such matter, but that it is a natural disease, say what you can they shall not believe you, but account you a Physician of small or no value, and whatsoever you do to them, it shall hardly do them any good at all, because of the fixedness of their depraved and prepossessed imagination.'

For our ancestors, the causes of neurological and psychiatric conditions such as epilepsy and schizophrenia were not known. Yet the symptoms, such as falling to the floor with a seizure for example, would have been all too apparent and with no causal frame of reference this must have been terrifying for all involved. Myth became the framework of understanding and elves served a very important, psychological purpose – they ensured that by identifying them as a cause then a solution could be determined.

Although the continuation of fairy beliefs is often thought to be peculiar to Scotland with archaeologist Leslie Grinsell saying for example that 'witch-lore and fairy-lore are often inextricably interwoven, especially in Scotland', the healing books of Mildþryþ demonstrate that this is not the case – elves were rampant in Hwicce territory. For Mildþryþ and her colleagues, elves were of very real concern. Often their behaviours were ill intended and caused sickness as this remedy from *Bald's Leechbook III* reveals:

> 'Wið ælfadle nim bisceopwyrt, finul elehtre, ælfþonan nioþowearde, ond gehalgodes cristes, mæles ragu, ond stor, do ælcre hand fulle, bebind ealle þa wyrta on claþe... gerec þone man mid þam wyrtum ær undern ond on niht... ond wyl on meolce... ond supe ær his mete, him biþ sona sel.'

> *'For elf-sickness, take bishopswort, fennel, lupin, the lower part of elfthon, lichen from the hallowed sign of Christ, and storax, take a handful of each, bind up all the plants in a cloth...smoke the man with the plants before morning and night...then boil them in milk...and let him sip it before food...it will soon be better for him.'*

Elves feature in many remedies from sixth century Hwicce country and these creatures are part of a more general category of 'fairy' folk that includes sprites, pixies, brownies and leprechauns. In Scotland the term fairy is most often used in the witch trials, but for the Hwicce and Anglo-Saxons, elves were the norm.

The above remedy could certainly be described today as exhibiting motifs of shamanism. First, there are herbs as we might expect but what follows is beyond the pharmaceutical. Lichen from a Christian cross shows inclusion of deific symbolism used to empower the remedy. More telling is the directive to smoke the patient with the herbs. Smoking or smudging is a traditional technique observed in surviving shamanic traditions today – the smoke from smouldering herbs is believed to cleanse a patient from malevolent energies that might be causing illness. There are many more cures in Mildþryþ's Old English healing books that deal with the unwanted attentions of elves.

It may simply be that a belief in fairies was retained in its original form for longer in Scotland and so survives into the trial materials when elves had died off in the minds of the English. It may also be true that scribes in the assizes of England were simply directed to change mentions of fairies and elves into spirits and demons causing these creatures to become lost within the accounts.

A second theme within trial testimony that exposes continuing shamanic traditions is the originating cause of cunning-women's healing abilities. The process whereby supernatural gifts appear to be ordained upon a human being is revealing, and we learn from accounts that usually a cunning-woman's abilities emerge from an initiating, traumatic personal event.

Bessie for example, had described how she encountered Tom Reid following a time of great personal stress and trauma. Ursula Kempe also explained during her trial that she had suffered from a lame leg and had sought out a cunning-woman to heal her. The cunning-woman had told Ursula that she needed to 'unwitch' herself, and to do this she would need to use hog's dung, charnel, sage and St John's Wort in a ritual. The remedy and ritual worked and Ursula's leg was cured. Following her healing, Ursula found that others began seeking her out, asking whether she could cure them of similar afflictions. At first Ursula simply told them to use the same remedy she had been given, but in time, she found she was able to cure other illnesses too and this was the beginning of her career as a cunning-woman.

Christiane Lewingston attested to being taught healing by the fairies following her daughter's illness and Jonet Boyman claimed she had been taught the healing arts by an unnamed cunning-woman from Potterrow who had originally performed a healing on her (Henderson, 2011).

A cunning-woman named Mette Pedersdatter from the village of Ulsted near Gøl was convicted of witchcraft in 1618. She had healed the sick, conducted counter-magic for those who had been cursed by malevolent magic and helped people whose cows had stopped producing milk. Mette was also gifted in exorcising spirits from people and she told the judiciary how a sorcerer had once sent an evil spirit to one of her patients. Mette, perhaps with some pride, described how she had managed to send the spirit back to the malevolent magic worker who had sent it.

When asked of the cause of her strange powers, Mette replied that she had been quite without them until an incident where she had died. She said that she had died for three days and three nights and had experienced heaven and hell. The nature of her death is unrecorded, but Mette was sure that this was the point when she received her gift. She was an intelligent woman and during her trial she even stated that she understood how her abilities at exorcising evil spirits, control of supernatural forces and her reputation for identifying illnesses and practicing counter-magic, was characteristic of those being convicted of witchcraft. Mette, it seems, knew her fate.

Doctor Hank Wesselman has explained how:

> 'the 'shamanic experience' almost always begins with some sort of personal crisis, often of epic proportions – an earth trembling, soul shaking, life altering spiritual emergence (or emergency) that can be utterly shattering – one that often looks a lot like mental illness to the Western medical world.'

Traumatic events or illnesses can cause momentary or acute experiences of dissociation where perception can alter. The phenomenological psychologist Mihaly Csikszentmihalyi described these occurrences as 'deep flow' experiences where action and awareness can merge resulting in a loss of ego with a corresponding 'kinaesthetic sensation'. On a day-to-day basis, we often have fleeting moments like these; driving on a familiar road and suddenly realising we have drifted off and no longer know exactly where we are, is one such moment. Escalate that experience a hundred-fold and the moment deepens to offer an opportunity to perceive and experience selfhood in relationship to the exterior world and sometimes, the divine, in a totally new way.

Joseph Campbell has investigated this loss or descent into the unconscious and views it as a powerful trigger in the initiatory path of the ancient shaman. Initiation enacts through ritual the loss of self experienced in deep trauma. It is designed to strip the candidate of all previous worldly egoic entrapments and bring forth the re-birthed, spiritually awakened, enlightened individual. This individual might then have an elevated, divinised or Christ consciousness.

Campbell describes how this crisis, whether welcomed through a ritual of initiation or as a spontaneous personal event, can often make or break an individual. It can be seen as a process that stands outside of the arena of everyday experience and for those ready or open enough to walk through the doorway that opens, it can be a highly transformative event. He goes further to describe the threshold, stating that most people speak of an encounter with what they may term a god, spirit, guardian, angel, force or protector. This spiritual being, 'may bestow power and knowledge upon the aspirant, but as a threshold guardian, part of its job is to turn back spiritual questers who are not yet ready to encounter that which lies beyond the doorway into the other worlds.' Campbell also said in one of his seminars that if a person is unable to recognise these guardians fully, then they are likely to interpret them as malevolent. Also, for those persons unready for any such experience 'the doorway remains closed'. It is then unfortunately the case, that the person will emerge with only their trauma and fear intact.

Beneath the bizarre transcripts of the European witch trials we find evidence for a continuation of ancient shamanic traditions and beliefs into the pre-Modern era. Yet increasingly it is emerging from more contemporary sources, that these ancient beliefs and the cunning-women who embodied them, may not have completely died out at all. Writing in 1807 Robert Southey commented that:

'a Cunning-Woman, as they are termed, is to be found near every town, and though the laws are occasionally put in force against them, still it is a gainful trade.'

It would seem therefore, that despite the 'laws', cunning-women were still in existence following the worst of the witch trials. In Yorkshire alone, historian Kathryn Smith has found thirty-nine accounts of cunning-women still practicing medicine throughout the nineteenth century. Even moving into the twentieth century the historian Arthur Norway commented in his *Highways and Byways of Devon and Cornwall*, (1911) that there were 'few towns or villages of any consequence,' that did not have a cunning-woman.

Epilogue

'Although magic has disappeared from the criminal codes of our time, the question of its legitimacy still persists as a moral, theological and also medical question.'

Anonymous, *Meditations on the Tarot*, 1980.

Witches should be wary in the Cotswolds today. Seven miles southeast from Mildþryþ's resting place is the little village of Lower Quinton. Opposite the church stands a picturesque thatched cottage, which in 1945 was home to a 74-year-old farm worker named Charles Walton. Ask about Charles in the village today and you will receive friendly smiles formed on tight lips. Small English villages are not accustomed to gruesome murders and even less familiar to those associated with witchcraft and blood sacrifice. When the BBC investigated the story in 2014, they were told by a local, 'No one will talk to you about it. The family have all gone now anyway. There are none of the Walton family left here now. I have no answers to your questions.'

It had been the evening of Valentine's Day when Charles was discovered near Meon Hill with a hedging hook through his throat and his neck pinned through to the ground with a pitchfork. A cross had been carved into the bare flesh of his chest. The scene was bloody. His throat was a gaping mess and his attacker had beaten him over the head with the walking stick old Charles used due to his rheumatism.

The murder was so unusual and brutal that the Chief Constable of Warwickshire called on the assistance of Scotland Yard. Two days later Chief Inspector Robert Fabian arrived in the small Cotswolds' village that was home to just 493 people. The detective was led the three quarters of a mile from Charles's cottage to the edge of the field where his body lay undisturbed, watched over by local police.

Motive was the immediate mystery. The old man was frail and carried no money or effects. He had been in the fields that day tending to the hedges, which was his common practice at the Firs farm. The case was never solved and in later years attracted the interest of a number of historians and researchers. Margaret Murray spent a week in Lower Quinton and concluded herself 'almost satisfied' that Charles's death was indeed linked to witchcraft. She said of the village that 'it is typical of those places where superstitions and beliefs in witchcraft still exist. One significant thing is that it occurred on St Valentine's Day – February the 14th. In the pre-Christian era from which many rituals still live, February was a sacrificial month.'

Historian Donald McCormick also investigated the murder and dedicated his resultant book *Murder by Witchcraft* to a vicar with the poignant words:

'With a special plea for white magic which, as the Renaissance Christians believed, is not so very far distant from the principles of Christianity and science.'

Even Fabian's associate Alec Spooner believed that witchcraft was involved. He writes of the landscape and spaces in that part of the Cotswolds and in particular of the standing circle known as the Rollright Stones (the whispering knights):

'On the hilltops around Lower Quinton are circles of stones where witches are reputed to hold Sabbaths, and it was under the shadow of Meon Hill, not far from the stone circle of whispering knights, that on Valentine's Day of 1945 a rheumaticky, gnarled old man was found murdered,'

The Rollright Stones and witchcraft are not mentioned in reports of the time, yet these ideas obviously haunted Spooner. Perhaps due to the unsettling knowledge that 'rheumaticky' Charles was not the first to be murdered in this peculiar way.

In 1875, 79-year-old Ann Tennant of Long Compton, which lies half a mile from the Rollrights, closer in fact than Lower Quinton, was found murdered in similar circumstances. She had, so it was stated, been pinned to the ground with a pitchfork and slashed through her throat with a bill-hook by a local named James Heyward. Heyward admitted that he had 'pinned her to the ground with a hayfork before slashing her throat with a bill-hook in the form of a cross'. Historian Clive Holland wrote in his book *Warwickshire*, that this was a way to kill witches that had been known locally for many centuries. The Anglo-Saxons he said, called it *stacung* (sticking). On the Ann's death certificate it states:

> 'Wilful Murder – Deliberately stabbed to death by James [Hayward] with a fork under a delusion of witchcraft.'

In a statement written in 1928, an eyewitness to the attack on Ann also spoke of witchcraft. Richard Clarke described that Ann was a suspected witch and that another local woman known as Granny Faulknew was also considered to be a witch as she could change into different animal forms. Also, according to the clergyman James Harvey Bloom, it was widely known that 'there are enough witches in Long Compton to draw a wagon of hay up Long Compton Hill' and that in the area generally, 'the influence of witches goes and comes like the full moon'.

Chief Inspector Fabian noted the villager's extreme reluctance to discuss the murder of old Charles. Arthur Evans, researching folklore in the area in 1875, speaks of a superstition that the locals had that if you spill the blood of a witch then her power disappears. This has led many to speculate that the murders were ritualistic, a kind of blood sacrifice to thwart the supposed evil of the suspected witch.

A case of attempted murder, also from 1875, might have inspired Evan's research; magistrates in Weston-super-Mare, Somerset, were perplexed to have before them an unrepentant 72-year-old woman named Hester Adams who had stabbed another woman, Maria Pring, in the face. Adams claimed during her trial that, 'I can prove that she is an old witch, and she hag-rided me and my husband for the past two years.' When asked what she meant by 'hag-rided' she replied, 'I have seen her many times at night, but she does not come bodily.' Instead, Adams explained that the accused visited her, 'in a nasty, evil, spiritual way, making a nasty noise.' Adams was convinced that the only way to break the witch's curse was to draw her blood, and so strong was her belief that she said, 'I'll draw it again for her if she does not leave me alone.' Hester Adams was fined one shilling.

A similar account of attempted murder occurred in 1867 when it was heard in the Warwickshire assizes that John Davis had attempted to murder Jane Ward, as he believed her to be a witch. During his testimony he too painted a colourful story of ghostly, hag-like apparitions visiting his home at night and bringing terror to his family – his daughter was tossed about the house like a doll and one of the spirits claimed to be none other than Saint Genevieve. Davis also stated that the first night of peace they had enjoyed in many was that immediately following his attack on Jane. This he explained, was because the spilling of her blood broke the curse.

Jane also gave testimony at the trial. Still bandaged from the attack where the accused had slashed her face with a knife, she relayed a story of consistent abuse from Davis and his family that had started a year earlier. They would shout 'witch' at her whenever they passed and on the night of the attack Davis's two sisters verbally abused her before their brother struck.

Jane survived her attack and lived at number 4, Emms Court, Sheep Street, Old Stratford. In the 1871 census she is 60-years-old and her occupation is as a charwoman. Her daughter Emma is 15-years-old and of the same employ. A William and Hannah Davis live at number one, both in their late seventies and possibly the parents of John who, Jane recounted, often walked past her door. By the next census in 1881, however, Jane and Emma have disappeared although Hannah Davis, now widowed, is still at number one.

Postscript

Accurate figures have never been satisfactorily ascertained for how many died in the witch craze. A general consensus finds around 200,000 people tortured and killed across Europe and 350 in North America – the English witch-finder Matthew Hopkins had 68 people put to death in Bury St. Edmunds and 19 people hanged in Chelmsford in a single day.

On 27 July 2004, the Queen pardoned eighty-one witches. Convicted and burnt in what Scottish historian Roy Pugh has described as a 'mini-holocaust', their crime was of using witchcraft to kill James I, and therefore their convictions were formally for treason. This offered a legal avenue for the Baron Gordon Prestoungrange to petition for their pardon, as under Scottish law, treason could not be proven by way of 'spectral evidence' or evil spirits. Therefore, the convictions were unsound. The Crown agreed and it was held that:

> 'both fact and law exist for vacating the conviction of all those persons and their cats who were convicted of 'conjuration or sorcery' within the jurisdiction of the Baron Courts of Prestoungrange and Dolphinstoun and executed for the same before the enactment of *The Witchcraft Act 1735*: In all cases such convictions were based upon 'spectral evidence' legally insufficient under Scots law to sustain a conviction.'

Here is a list of those pardoned. The names of the cats, also killed, have not survived:

Name	Year of Execution
Margaret Aitchesoun	1590
Masle Aitchesoun	1590
Agnes Aird	1661
Marjorie Andersone	1678

POSTSCRIPT

Margaret Auchinmoutie	1661
Marioun Ballzie (Baillie)	1590
Christian Blaikie	1661
Meg Bogtoun	1590
Janet Boyd	1628
Bessie Broune (Brown)	1590
Thomas Brounhill (Brownhill)	1590
Wife of Thomas Brounhill	1590
Duncan Buchquhannan	1590
Margaret Butter	1661
Martha Butter	1659
Jonett Campbell	1590
Elspeth Cheuslie	1679
Thomas Cockburn	1590
Marioun Congilton	1590
Bessie Cowane	1590
Beatrix Cuthbertson	1628
Janet Darlig	1628
Agnes Dempstar	1628
Gelie Duncan	1591
Catherine Duncane	1590
Thomas Fean	1591
John Flan or Flene	1590
Jonett Gall	1590
Malie Geddie	1590
Helen Gibesone (Gibson)	1661
Johnne Gordon	1590
Catherene Gray	1590
Jonnett Gray	1661
Robert Griersoune	1591
Issobell Griersoune	1607
Issobell Gylloun	1590
Margaret Hall	1661
Agnes Kelly	1678
Cristian Kerington	1590
Helene Lauder	1590
Issobell Lauder	1590
Agnes Liddell	1628
Katherine Liddell	1678

Jonett Logan	1590
Ewfame McCalzean	1590
Euphernia McLean	1590
Catherine McGill	1590
Gilbert McGill	1590
Johnne McGill	1590
Barbara Mathie	1628
Wife of George Moitis	1590
Wife of Nichol Murray	1590
Ane Nairn	1591
Jonett Nicolsoun	1590
Marioun Nicolsoun	1590
Margaret Oliver	1628
Marie Patersoune	1590
Wife Portar of Seton	1590
Helen Quhyte (White)	1590
Alexander Quhytelaw (Whitelaw)	1590
Wife of John Ramsey	1590
Marion Ranking	1590
Janet Reid	1628
Bessie Riddell	1628
Margaret Ridpeth	1628
Donald Robinson	1590
Anny Rycheson	1590
Daughters of Agnes Sampsoun	1590
Agnes Sampsoun	1590
Marioune Schaw	1590
Ane Simson	1591
Wife of Smythe	1590
Elizabeth Steven	1629
Jonett Straitton	1590
Janet Strauchane (Strachan)	1628
Margrett Thomson	1590
Bessie Thomsoune	1590
Katherine Wallace	1590
Charles Wat	1591
Bessie Wrycht (Wright)	1590
Margaret Young	1628

Bibliography

ALLEN, J., *The Art of Medicine in Ancient Egypt*, (Yale University Press. 2005).

BRIGGS, R., *Witches and Neighbours: The Social and Cultural Context of European Witchcraft*, (Oxford, Wiley-Blackwell, 1997).

BUCCOLA, R., *Fairies, Fractious Women, and the Old Faith* (Susquehanna University Press, 1 July 2006).

CAMPBELL, J., *The Masks of God: Occidental Mythology: Occidental Mythology,* (Penguin, 26 Mar. 1992).

COATES, R., *The name of the Hwicce: A discussion.* (The University of West England, 2013).

CROSS, F., *Canaanite Myth and Hebrew Epic*, (Harvard University Press; New Ed edition, 1 Sept. 1997).

DURANT, W., *Caesar and Christ*, (Blackstone Audio, 2014).

ECKARDT, H., *Objects and Identities: Roman Britain and the North-western Provinces*, (OUP, 2014).

FOUCAULT, M., *Madness and Civilisation: a history of insanity in the Age of Reason*, (Tavistock Publications, 1971).

GOODARE, J., *The European Witch-Hunt*, (Routledge; 1 edition, 1 Dec. 2010).

HAWKES, S., *The Anglo-Saxon Cemetery at Finglesham, Kent*, (Oxford University School of Archaeology Monograph, 27-Apr-2006).

HENDERSON, L., *History of Everyday Life in Medieval Scotland*, (Edinburgh University Press, 6 Jun. 2011).

HENDERSON, L., *Scottish Fairy Belief: A History*, (Tuckwell Press Ltd; 2nd edit. John Donald 2007 edition, 1 Mar. 2001).

HENDERSON, L., *Detestable Slaves of the Devil': Changing Attitudes to Witchcraft in Sixteenth-Century Scotland in A History of Everyday Life in Medieval Scotland, 1000 to 1600. Vol. 1.* (Edinburgh University Press, 2011).

HIGHAM, N. and **RYAN, M.**, 2013, *The Anglo-Saxon World* , (Yale University Press, 14 Jun. 2013).

HINES, J., *The Scandinavian character of Anglian England in the pre-Viking,* (British Archaeological Reports, 1 July 1984).

JAMES NAPIER, J., *Western Scottish Folklore & Superstitions*, (Lethe Press, 1 Dec. 2008).

KARRAS, R., *Common Women: Prostitution and Sexuality in Medieval England,* (Oxford University Press USA; New Ed edition, 1 Jan. 1996).

LEYSER, H., *Medieval Women: Social History Of Women In England 450-1500,* (W&N; New Ed edition, 1 Sept. 2005).

MACLEOD, S., *The Divine Feminine in Ancient Europe: Goddesses, Sacred Women and the Origins of Western Culture,* (McFarland & Co, 30 Dec. 2013).

MAGEDANZ, S., *Cliffs Notes on St. Augustine's Confessions,* (Cliffs Notes; 1 edition (19 Mar. 2004).

MAGENNIS, H., *The Cambridge Introduction to Anglo-Saxon Literature,* (Cambridge University Press, 2011).

MAXWELL-STUART, P., *Satan's Conspiracy: Magic and Witchcraft in Sixteenth-century Scotland,* (Tuckwell Press Ltd, 1 Nov. 2000).

OPIE, I., and **TATUM, M.,** *A Dictionary of Superstitions,* (OUP, 1989).

RAFFEL, B., *Poems and Prose from the Old English,* (Yale University Press, 1998).

REESE-TAYLOR, K., *Sacred Places and Sacred Landscapes,* (The Oxford Handbook of Mesoamerican Archaeology, 2012).

REYNOLDS, A., *Anglo-Saxon Deviant Burial Customs* (OUP, Medieval History and Archaeology, 2014).

RUSSELL MOCK, S., *Say What I am Called: A Corpus of Anglo-Saxon Self-Referential Inscriptions,* (University of Oregon, 2016).

SCOTT, W., *Letters on Demonology and Witchcraft* (Myth, Legend & Folklore, (Wordsworth Editions Ltd, GB (2001).

SCULL, A., *Museums of Madness: The Social Organisation of Insanity in Nineteenth Century England* (Penguin Books; New e. edition, 1 Sept. 1982).

STENTON, F., *Anglo-Saxon England* (Oxford history of England, 1970).

STEWART-WILLIAMS, S., and **PODD, J.,** *The Placebo Effect: Dissolving the Expectancy Versus Conditioning Debate,* (Psychological Bulletin Copyright 2004 by the American Psychological Association, Inc. 2004, Vol. 130, No. 2).

SMITH, M., *The Origins of Biblical Monotheism: Israel's Polytheistic Background and the Ugaritic Texts,* (Oxford University Press, U.S.A.; New Ed edition, 2003).

THOMAS WRIGHT, T., *Narratives of Sorcery and Magic: From the Most Authentic Sources,* (Ulan Press, 31 Aug. 2012).

WATTS, A., *Easter: its Story and Meaning,* (Henry Schuman, 1950).

Index

INDEX